REVIVAL IN THE PEWS

Uncovering the Plot to Destroy Your Destiny

Vivian Phillips Johnson

REVIVAL IN THE PEWS:
Uncovering the Plot to Destroy Your Destiny
By Vivian Phillips Johnson

The Royal Court Publishing
Phoenix, Arizona
www.theroyalcourtpublishing.com

Usage Rights:
All Scripture quotations are taken from the New King James Bible unless otherwise indicated.

Back Cover Photo by: Rochelle (Roc) Wilson

CONTENT

DEDICATION

This book is dedicated to my little sister, Valeria (Neicey) Denise Davis (1964-2012), and the estimated 1.76 billion un-discipled Believers like her, who sit on the pew, wanting to fulfill their destiny, but do not know how—and nobody is teaching them.

We miss you Neiceybug, Smurf, Baby Girl, Bugsy, Mishababy! You fought the best fight you could. Though you went to Church regularly and never became a disciple, you still kept the faith. Now you can rest!

Acknowledgements

"Sometimes, it takes a village to write a book." Vivian Johnson

Fredric D. Johnson, thank you for the freedom and your support to write this book. You are truly appreciated. **Tawana,** thank you for your unconditional love and spiritual guidance. **Jenene**, my Senior Publisher, thank you for coaching me to excellence and managing my tantrums. **BilliJoy,** my editor, Editing Addict, LLC, your patience and grace to edit this book was stellar.

Brother Michael W. Smith and Karen, Kelley and the Hardcore Christianity/House of Healing family (Anthony, Corrina, Diane, Joe, Karen K., Nikole, Paula, Pastor Francis, Rick, Robert, Ron, Tony, Val, and Wayne) the harvest truly is plentiful. Brother Michael, your tireless labor to help people tormented by spirits makes you a true Shepherd. You and Kelley are the reason I continue to grow in deliverance ministry. It is an honor to serve with you and your team Bro. Michael.

To the **Believers Behind Bars**: Ddevin (my nephew), Troney, Sam, Isaiah, and James. These Men of God prayed and fasted as I wrote this book. It is a privilege to walk with you.

The **Scipio-Turner Family Prayer Call** participants (Auntie Queen, Carl, Caroline, Darrell, Diane, Jeanette, Lisa, Lora, Paulette and Don) Your encouragement and prayers over this endeavor are priceless.

My Best Friend Forever, Marlene (www.luvmyartbymwilson.com) her husband Rochelle (Roc), and my dear friend Jann: while writing this book you opened your homes and hearts and offered comfort. I am grateful to have people like you in my life. Thank you eternally!

Hortencia, *Mi Amiga*, and twin flame. You have a heart for Mexico and mine is for Africa, because we know God has not forgotten them. Thank you for always sharing. May God be the strength of your heart royal Daughter of the King!

To my **Beta Readers** (Anthony, Arnie and Kelly, Diane, Kathryn, Paula, Pastor Harris, Sam, Tawana, Michael W. Smith and Karen) your feedback on the overall content of this book gave me hope. Thank you for your time and help.

Pastor James L. Harris and the **New Hope Church of the Living God** family. Thank you.

Abba's Writers, led by BilliJoy, Madison, and April. The Rough Draft pre-screenings, your red critiques, encouragement, training, and grooming was right on time. I am a better writer and a more equipped author because of all of you, thank you.

To everyone who answered my many requests for prayer. You did more than you will ever know. Thank you, and may God richly bless you for your sacrifice.

R   E   V   I   V   A   L
May you be engulfed by the spirit of Revival!

According to GotQuestions.org *"Revival* refers to a spiritual reawakening from a state of dormancy or stagnation in the life of a believer. It encompasses the resurfacing of a love for God, an appreciation of God's holiness, a passion for His Word and His church, a convicting awareness of personal and corporate sin, a spirit of humility, and a desire for repentance and growth in righteousness. Revival invigorates and sometimes deepens a believer's faith, opening his or her eyes to the truth in a fresh, new way. It generally involves the connotation of a fresh start with a clean slate, marking a new beginning of a life lived in obedience to God."[1]

PRAY BEFORE READING THIS BOOK

Father, I believe having this book in my hands is a sign of your love. I know you want the best for me, and for that I am grateful.

Forgive me for everything I have not done to walk in my true destiny, including reading and studying my Bible, being connected to your church, and telling people about you. Remove every hindrance to me reaching my full spiritual potential.

As I turn these pages, reveal hidden agendas, expose demonic plots, unmask the little foxes, and give me the revelation I need to succeed. Guard my heart; open my eyes and ears to what will transform my life as I go from section to section. Leave no stone unturned.

Help me Lord when I feel convicted, and give me the patience to continue, and the wisdom to take action where appropriate. I want to overcome every obstacle and be victorious on all levels. I cast down each distraction as it comes to sabotage me from finishing this book.

Console me when I am overwhelmed, and guide me into all truth. Bind any demonic spirits operating in me —including the seducing and unclean spirits, the lying spirits, the deaf and dumb spirits, or the spirits of fear, deception, mental confusion, and witchcraft.

Protect me from my adversaries and keep your hedge sure. I command rejection and/or abandonment to go, and I welcome the spirit of wisdom and understanding, counsel and might, knowledge and fear of the Lord.

Fill me with your love and stir up revival in me as you open the eyes of my heart to truth and revelation for my future. I am ready to do whatever is necessary to impact the lives of those attached to me walking in my destiny. I receive all you have for me in the name of Jesus. Amen

WARNING

This book may have consequences and/or side effects not covered in this warning. Also, debating this book with people who only practice religious tradition will weaken its potency.

This book...
- Will bless your heart
- Reduces emotional drama experienced at church
- Relieves spiritual constipation
- Is an antibiotic for spiritual blindness and deceptive practices
- Eliminates chronic procrastination from only sitting in the pew
- Exposes the work of the enemy
- Contains strong language
- Will expose sin
- May encourage you to pray for the sick
- Can stimulate inner healing and/or deliverance
- Encourages forgiveness of yourself and others
- Is written to spark revival in your life

IMPORTANT NOTICE: Once you read this book, continued denial of the truth could be hazardous to your health.

DISCLAIMER: The information in this book focuses on the specific issue of only going to church and doing nothing else including growing. It is not intended to cover all possible scenarios or everything a Christian needs to know about the subject. For the full scope of how to live as a Believer, please refer to your Bible.

PREFACE
Why I Wrote this Book

The un-timely death of my baby sister, Neicey—who went to church regularly, but never matured—is what gave me the idea to write this book. What compelled me to get it done was my observations and frustrations with the growing number of unequipped Christians desperate for help, who are sitting in our pews, and not getting it. Not to mention, I was one of them.

I had no peace knowing Neicey did not fulfill the dream in her heart to tell the world how awesome God had been to her and her children. Every time I came to visit, she would share how she wanted to proclaim the Good News of God's grace. She felt like she had a lot to say considering she had been through so much.

We are outraged, at least some of us are, about the European slave-trade atrocity where over twelve million Africans were stolen from their homes and families, and sent to various parts of the world. We lament over the injustice of the Jewish Holocaust where six million Jews (one and a half million children), were persecuted for their faith and heinously murdered in inhumane ways.

Now, in modern society we are watching history repeat itself. The greatest spiritual Holocaust of all time is underway in the life of every Believer who is not growing. Up to 80% of the Body of Christ is un-discipled, which is the equivalent of more than 1.7 billion Christians.

The lack of discipleship is having a profound effect on individual Believers and their families—certainly our churches as a whole, the communities we live in, our cities, and the entire world. The elephant sitting in the middle of Christendom has to be talked about otherwise, fulfilling your destiny will be difficult, if not almost impossible.

About the Book

My mission with this book is to empower the people sitting idle in the pews by educating them on basic Kingdom protocol, practice, and behavior.

Eventually moving them from inactive Christians in the pew to activated Disciples in the promise, who are maturing in their faith.

This book provides direction to a chosen people who can change the world. It will dispel the lies of the Enemy, and expose his vicious plot, while offering solutions to those who want them, and educating and releasing those willing.

The information herein is a spiritual antibiotic similar to Vancomycin, a medicine given as a "drug of last resort." The state of the Body is past oral remedies and time is very short as we truly are in the last days. The dismal condition of the sheep warrants a supernatural intravenous application directly into the vein. We need renewed minds that are not compromised by fear, institutional resistance, biblical ignorance, or spiritual perversion.

Each segment will triage the cancer of complacency, codependency, and religious routine that hinders the potential of millions of Christians, who are the key to reaching the unsaved souls whose lives hang in the balance.

The religious practice of only sitting in the pews is a widespread epidemic aggressively undermining the real plan of God. As you go through this alliteration of The Problem, The Plot, The Players, The Plan and The Promise, which is culminated by The Commissioning, it will expose the darkness fueling this plague, and then guide you into victory over it.

I am His Servant and an oracle of God's love; I am called to carry this message of hope on a platform of truth for Christians who want the fullness of their inheritance. If there is any failure in this endeavor to uncover the plot of the enemy and ignite revival in the heart of God's people, it would be mine, not God's.

Hungry, but un-discipled Christians, who thirst for righteousness will be filled. The millions of disgruntled and disenfranchised prodigal sons and daughters, who fled the flock, will read this book and understand why they were so easily severed from the assembly, and they will come home. Discipled Believers, of which there are few, will be empowered to duplicate themselves. Then, Neicey's life will not have been in vain, after all. Now you know why I wrote this book.

When you see this flame or **DISCIPLE ME NOW**:

- Learn – Read and study the Bible
- Grow –Mature in righteousness
- Practice – Put into action
- Go – Get off the pew, share, and multiply

How you approach the fire is critical to your destiny. Posture yourself to be engulfed by revival. Be teachable and do not procrastinate. Embrace the knowledge and wisdom with humility.

This book is grounded in truth, righteousness, and the prophetic, which should expose and uproot deception. Do not wrestle against the process, even when it is uncomfortable. The Kingdom of God is coming to earth, and the only way it is going to come, is through you.

Abundant Blessings Beloved

"Those who do nothing while witnessing injustice and wrong-doing, do worse than those who commit acts of injustice."
— **Martin Luther King, Jr.**

INTRODUCTION
It's Resurrection Time

In March of 2012, my baby sister Neicey flew to Phoenix to visit our family. She died two days later. Neicey always did whatever she wanted to do, no matter what anybody else said or thought. Her little body could not take the beatings that diabetes was giving her, and flying only made it worse.

Neicey had more to contribute, and it saddened me she did not get that chance. It was even more devastating to think there are millions and millions of Christians in the same predicament, and they too will die unfulfilled if something does not change. Although that is tragic, it is catastrophic to ponder the absence of their spiritual impact on the world.

When I did Neicey's eulogy, it gave me a glimpse of revival and the hindrances to it, which had everything to do with why she did not grow spiritually. As we prepared for Neicey's home-going, there was a lot happening that had my heart in conflict.

Jesus died for us to have abundant life (John 10:10). He said we can lay hands on the sick and they will recover. So, what was the problem? Why was our little Neiceybug laying in a casket at forty-eight with an unfulfilled destiny and body riddled with long-term infirmities?

Once I gathered myself from the devastating news of Neicey passing, I sought God for direction on trying to raise her from the dead. The Lord pressed on my heart there would be a resurrection. It was all I needed to hear, and from that moment, I had a one-track mind.

This was my opportunity to do what Jesus said we could do and who better to do it with than my dead baby sister? But, first I had to get to Phoenix.

Considering this was my inaugural dead-raising attempt, I did not have a playbook on how to do it. What I am about to share may sound crazy, but it did not feel that way at the time. I was driven by love, the same love that drove

Jesus to raise Lazarus, his friend, from the dead when he had been expired for three days. Jesus loved Lazarus and I loved my sister and I did not want to see her children motherless like me.

There were many obstacles I had to face and overcome, including the guy at the mortuary, who didn't want to give me access to my sister. He obviously did not realize *no* was not an option. The destiny pinned on me, before there was ever a people group, was unfolding and nothing was going to stop it. Finally, he relented, and put Neicey in the viewing room. We were about to witness a miracle.

Faith Never Fails

There she was, wrapped in a white blanket that gave her no warmth. Her body was cold and stiff. As I looked at my little sister laying there, my heart must have doubled in size. There was no doubt she would get up; she had to.

It was time to bring Heaven to Earth, but first we needed to pray. In short, we began to command, call forth, decree, repeat Scriptures, and nothing was working. My only hope was that, my cousin and I were on one accord, and looking back, I do not think we were.

Next, I did something drastic. In the recesses of my mind, I remembered reading in the Bible about someone using a staff to try to raise the dead. Well, I brought one with me from San Diego. I waived my wooden staff over her body and commanded the spirit of death to let her go, nothing.

Now Gehazi went on ahead of them, and laid the staff on the face of the child; but there was neither voice nor hearing (2 Kings 4:31)

As a last-ditch effort, I did what Elisha did (2 Kings 4:34-35), well almost. If by faith he could lay his body on a dead boy and it gave him life I would do nothing less. Scripture said I had the same power in me that Elisha had in him. So, I laid my Spirit-filled body across hers and she still didn't move.

Nothing would distract me, including the funeral-home director peering at me from the back of the room. Fear was not my friend, and doubt was my enemy. Neither would seduce me to leave the narrow path I was compelled to walk. The first attempt may not have worked, but it was not over.

Two Times a Charm

The second time I tried to raise Neicey from the dead was at the funeral home in Milwaukee. Nothing I did was planned. There was no script. My actions were not premeditated. But, I was determined in my heart to see the Word of God fulfilled.

Nobody from Phoenix told the family in Milwaukee what I tried to do. It was good I only had one witness, and to my knowledge she kept quiet. The mortuary in Phoenix called the mortuary in Milwaukee to warn them that a crazy woman was coming, and that crazy woman would be me. Seriously, why would someone who is doing what Jesus told us to do be considered crazy? Personally, I think it is crazy that we do not even try.

Sometimes, we have to shake off what other people think, and keep going. I shook it off and focused on making sure Neicey was presentable for viewing. The only concern I had was what would happen to her clothes when she came back to life and stood up.

Somebody had to do Neicey's hair, because the beautician did not show up, and that somebody turned out to be me. Neicey would pitch a fit if she was resurrected in front of a crowd and her hair was a hot mess. This time my attempt to raise her was not as dramatic as Phoenix, but I was just as invested. Once again, she still layed there breathless.

Holding On to The Promise

There are no words to explain the conviction in me to try one last time. If the word God had given me was going to happen, it would have to be at her celebration. I did not want her to go home to God. I wanted her to come back to us.

God does everything decent and in order for a reason, so I had to make sure when she climbed out of her casket her clothes wouldn't fall off. If they did she would be madder than a cat squirted with water.

The night before Neicey's service, Father gave me the order and content of her eulogy. It was obvious what was going to happen, but I was focused on her being resurrected. Once we arrived at the church, I inform the pastor what I was going to do. Next, I gave the funeral-home attendants instructions. One of them sneeringly told me I could not pray a resurrection prayer over my sister. The religiously opposed were hell bent on working my nerves.

The spiritual ignorance I was encountering was giving me grief. I would not be beguiled by distractions of any kind. My fellow brothers and sisters in Christ were operating like they had Tasers and I was their perpetrator. Their aggressive reactions and responses did not line up with biblical truths. People seemed to be okay with Neicey being dead, and I felt exactly the opposite. Each step toward raising her echoed I was on a team of two—God and me—and for me that was enough.

If God is for us, who can be against us (Romans 8:31)

Well, everything was in order. The viewing was over and the casket was closed. Once all the ministers were seated on the pulpit, the service began. When it was my turn to speak, I walked to the podium and began the sermon I was given. Low and behold, a fully engulfed fire was brewing inside me.

My instructions were to help the people understand death was never in His plan. Neither was sickness part of His promise. As an afterthought, I now realize He was building our faith for the supernatural demonstration about to take place.

Next, I uttered the words that would shake and silence the whole building, "Open it!" The funeral-home attendants rushed from the back of the church as I was making my way to the casket. Once it was opened, I was standing in front of it with anticipation.

My back was to the audience so I had no visual on the commotion, and neither did I see my cousins who ran out of the church. Apparently, folks started standing up around the room and some even voiced using the nearby widows as an exit if Neicey got up. One of my cousins said he felt pulled onto his feet.

His wife next to him asked what he was doing.

He told me, "I couldn't help it."

They raised the lid on Neicey's casket. Every eye left in the room was glued to that ugly gray box. If curiosity alone could have drawn her forth, she would have risen up. I stood there in full confidence this was the moment. Not an ounce of doubt, no fear—only complete assurance in the Father who sent me.

Neicey was about to be reunited with her precious children, our family, and the friends who cherished her. It was exciting to think she would be fully healed in her body and free of the torment and brutality of Type One diabetes and all the complications that came with it.

God would not raise her with the sickness that took her away from us still ravishing her body. My mind said her pancreas would start releasing the insulin she desperately needed. Her kidneys, that were lifeless without dialysis, would clean her blood and she would lose the shadow of death that lay on top of her skin. Her heart that kept attacking would rejoice in being restored.

Maybe we would even experience a few creative miracles and she would come back with the toes that were amputated and twenty-twenty vision, because Lord knows that girl could not see.

When Neicey was about seventeen or eighteen, she started losing her eyesight to diabetes. My mom prayed for God to heal her and He did; Neicey got her sight back with no problems for over twenty years. It never dawned on me I was walking in a family legacy of supernatural exploits, until I wrote this book.

The room was a backdrop of complete silence as I stood with my hand on her chest calling her forth. Unfortunately, there was no sign of her returning. I walked back into the pulpit and said, Praise God, it does not appear it is going to be Neicey today who is raised from the dead. Somebody out there is going to experience the resurrection power of Jesus Christ. Turn to your neighbor and say, "It's resurrection time."

Unbeknownst to me, God had other plans. It was not Neicey that God was using me to pursue. While I thought He was finally going to let me raise someone from the dead, what I know in hindsight is He was guiding my actions toward the living dead, who needed revival in the pews.

It wasn't until after I exhausted every option to raise her did I see what God's plan was from the beginning. Sometimes we have to fall out of alignment with routine to access our destiny. Little did I know seeing the living-dead be revived was going to change my life, forever.

After the sermon, I was told some of my Christian family members thought I was crazy for what I did, and you might be thinking the same thing. One of my relatives asked if I was practicing witchcraft. Others questioned if my behavior of dead-raising was scriptural. And, with each comment I wondered if we were reading the same Bible.

Christians were talking so loud behind my back, I could hear them in the Spirit. Every step of faith I took, I was battling Believers, and that was painful.

My Bible said Jesus raised the dead, and told us we could do it too. Why is there such resistance to following in His steps?

One of the most courageous times of my Christian life was to continue to walk in faith when Neicey did not get up. I believed, without a doubt, what God said—to me directly and in His Word. Although my interpretation was wrong, the end result was not. But, all the drama left me perplexed.

On the flip side, people in attendance did not see what I saw when the people who were un-churched followed me home pleading for me to pray for them. They were not there when the phone rang off the hook with folks wanting copies of the service to share with their families. One of my relatives said, "If everyone in the room had the kind of faith you did, Neicey would have gotten up." Another cousin said, "I've only seen faith like that in the Bible."

Three of my cousins came to me immediately after the service to say they accept their call to the ministry. Clearly, Neicey's little home-going service paraded in the undeniable presence and power of God and it was causing the people to be revived.

Neicey's funeral was my intersection for destiny, where tragedy and faith collided. Even though I was under attack from all directions, I did not faint. The enemy had to be in the corner laughing at what he was doing, and enjoying those he was using to do it. Now, this book is payback.

Not long after Neicey's passing, I went on a retreat with Apostle Doctor Judy Bauer, the founder of Kingdom Advancement Ministries (KAM). KAM is a New Testament evangelism and discipleship-training program in Temecula, California, thriving in over forty nations. She shared the blueprint God gave her to make disciples and teach them how to multiply, which is what I was missing.

Over that weekend, I could not help but think Neicey never got to multiply. After we put Neicey to rest, I overcame the doubting Thomases, and the religious rhetoric of the unbelieving Believers, and reflected on what happened. It was clear. I had to tell as many Christians as I could what nobody told Neicey about maturing in her faith, how to multiply once she did—and why people may not be fulfilling their destiny.

"In a time of deceit, telling the truth is a revolutionary act."
— **George Orwell**

Section I

The Problem
Know the Problems and Practices That Hinder
A Kingdom-Driven Lifestyle

THE PROBLEM

You matter! Not only do you matter, what you are created to do matters. It matters to God, and it should matter to His people. Unfortunately, more often than not, it appears it does not, and therein is one of the problems in the Church. However, it is not the biggest problem we face in the Body of Christ.

My baby sister, Neicey, was like most Christians. She attended church regularly even though she was not actively involved. Something inside of all of us instinctively knows the answer is in the Church.

Week after week, month after month, and year after year, she sat on the pew. Neicey wore out her share of pews just like some of you. She propped her short behind, on those seats, like a happy little sheep.

At every church she attended, it was important to her to connect with the pastor. She thought she had a right to engage his or her shepherding skills, no matter what time of day or night it was. Is it not the pastor's responsibility to tend to the sheep? Or, is it?

She depended on the pastor giving her a word of encouragement, and maybe some guidance, during the many down times she encountered. Neicey wanted her life to matter, like most people do, even in the face of having generational diabetes, which limited her abilities.

It was easy for my sister to go to church, because we were raised to go. When we grew up we knew we were going every Sunday. Nobody asked us if we wanted to go, the way parents are with their children today. We went, and we had to have a good attitude about it. The thought of not going was not an option.

Back in the day, parents knew going to church or sending us was like good medicine. Has that priceless nugget been lost to a younger generation? Our grandparents went to church. They took our parents, and our parents took us.

Now we are taking our children, and their children—well, some of us. We have learned well the practice of going to church. Sadly, that may be where our learning stopped. It has been reported that perhaps over fifty percent of people who go to church are not even Christians.[2] If we took those statistics seriously, it should shift the way we do church.

Neicey was old school when it came to church, which means she dressed up. Today, almost anything goes. It was instilled in us when we went to God's House we wore our best. Now we focus on being politically correct and seeker-friendly. Does not matter if your breasts are hanging out, your dress is bootylicious, or your jeans are too tight? Now days we even have to risk looking at a man's underwear.

Not wearing clothes that would cause another person to stumble does not appear to be important anymore. The moral decline of our society has unequivocally made its way into our pews, and that certainly is a problem.

Going to church was a ritual for Neicey, even when she spent days before bedridden in a hospital. She would get up and go. For some, we go to God's house on Sunday, and raise a ton of hell on Monday, drink and cuss on Tuesday, dishonor our parents on Wednesday, and the rest of the week follows suit. Does it matter what we do every other day of the week?

We could not count the number of times Neicey literally walked out of the Intensive Care Unit (ICU) and into a pew. She would be in critical condition one day, leave the ICU, and go straight to work, church, or even to get her hair done. It was crazy, but we could not stop her, and it was probably good we did not succeed at trying.

She got her fix at church, and going made her feel better. It was like some of the drugs we take or the vices we have. Although short-lived, we are better for the moment, which is what most of us think. Church should be the place where we can go to get refreshed, empowered, and equipped to do the work of the ministry—or has it become something else?

In the midst of all her Church Going, Neicey did not get equipped for ministry or her destiny. People are showing up, but they have no idea what they should be doing with their lives once they lift off the pew, and maybe that is the problem.

For a short period, Neicey was married. She was a struggling single parent, dealing with an absentee father, and raising two children in the inner city of Milwaukee, Wisconsin. If we profiled her as a parishioner, she would fall into the category of high maintenance, low income, and sporadic attendance due to a chronic illness.

While she would not be considered the desirable church member to society, Jesus compelled the less fortunate to come. He said in Romans 15:1, *We then who are strong ought to bear with the scruples of the weak, and not to please ourselves.* Jesus died for people like Neicey.

Diabetic Diva

Neicey was a Type One brittle diabetic, which means her diabetes was extremely hard to control, and her medical drama was ever growing, and never-ending. It was so difficult to manage, she became her own physician. She rearranged the slogan "physician, heal thyself" to "patient, heal thyself." She started telling her doctors what to do to help her, and it worked!

On one of her many emergency-room excursions, the doctor informed us the slew of medicines were keeping her alive. He wanted her to sign a Do Not Resuscitate (DNR), but she would not. Neicey nicely informed all of us she was not about to die, and she was right. We, on the other hand, did not think she would make it through the upcoming Thanksgiving holiday.

During one of my visits home, we called the ambulance because Neicey's blood sugar plummeted to ten, and she was still conscious. By the time we got her to the Emergency Room, it had spiked to over 1200, and Neicey was still talking. Everybody was shocked. Nobody had ever seen anyone conscious with a blood sugar that high. But, Neicey had a habit of defying medicine.

Actually, she was so good at it, Marquette University Medical Center would invite her down to their campus to probe her unpredictable condition. It thrilled her to the moon because she wanted to tell them how special she was.

For many years, before she passed, Neicey was a very sick woman who was getting worse. The hospital was her secret lover, who she rendezvoused with too many times to count. Neicey was the typical Christian. She knew God healed, but how He did it escaped the un-discipled child of the King.

She always talked about being healed, but she did not know how to apprehend God's promises, let alone possess the Kingdom. She lived in a constant state of hope deferred, and dreams unfulfilled—like many of you reading this book—and without a doubt, that is a problem.

It became the norm to see Neicey being put in an ambulance. Even the drivers knew her and her children by name. Everyone in the Emergency Room knew her. She was in the hospital so much she often had the same room.

She would get discharged, and it appeared she sub-leased the space. Etched in her head was room 502, where she had so many near-death experiences. After a while, the family stopped counting.

Neicey passed away a few years ago of complications from her diabetes, and it was one of the saddest days of my life. It is still hard for me to believe my baby sister is gone. When I did her eulogy, I added up the miracles I knew for sure she had experienced—most of the children who were diagnosed with Type One Diabetes when she was died by the time they were twenty-five.

I calculated the number of days Neicey lived after twenty-five as a miracle. She got over 8300 another-day life miracles. I threw in a few extra for all the car accidents she had, when no one got hurt. She even hydroplaned over a fire hydrant, and walked away without a scratch.

Then I added some more for the many times she passed out in the bank, at the grocery store, in school, at work, or at home, and she did not kill herself collapsing to the floor. It was a good thing she was short, so she did not have far to fall.

Our little diva was never taught how to walk in faith for her healing as a Believer. She did not get the by-His-stripes-we-are-healed classes. However, she got a ton of sermons. I am sure if she had known a sermon is not enough to make a disciple, she would have wanted something more than what she got.

One time, Neicey and my oldest brother, John, came to visit me in Phoenix. On the flight back home, Neicey's blood sugar dropped because she fell asleep and forgot to eat. She slipped into a diabetic coma for the umpteenth time.

John got off the plane and Neicey was not behind him. Shortly after, here comes the Diabetic Diva laid out on a stretcher. Neicey passed out anywhere and everywhere. No place was off limits for her sporadic comas. Neicey may have never made it into the limelight, but she could sure create enough drama to put herself center stage. Sometimes, I think that little woman got a kick out of it too.

The biggest problem Neicey faced was not her tumultuous medical problems, although they were daunting, consuming, and outright inconvenient to the person who had to come to her rescue. She gave new meaning to "it takes a village."

It was not that she was a single parent raising two children in the inner city on government assistance, and with limited resources. Neither was it her inability to keep a job because she kept getting sick before her ninety-day probation period ended.

Neicey's problem is the same problem that many Christians face today. We are taught to go to church, not how to be the church. She needed to know how to become a Disciple, and then how to make disciples who multiplied, bringing the Kingdom of Heaven to Earth as we go.

One Life Matters

Everything that happens to you matters. It really does. When people do not think they matter it is a problem. It is a problem for them, for the Church, and it is an even bigger dilemma for the world. The Bible makes it very clear in John 13:35, which says, "*Your love for one another will prove to the world that you are my disciples* (NLT)." God intended for His people to be the solution, especially to those in the family of God.

> *Therefore, as we have opportunity, let us do good to all,*
> *especially to those who are of the household of faith (Galatians 6:10)*

It should be a top priority for the Body of Christ to make sure people know we care and they matter. Have you ever heard the saying: "actions speak louder than words?" You are important to God because He sent His only Son, Jesus—perfect in every way—to create a path for you back to Him. He wants to bless you with His goodness all the days of your life, because you matter that much.

It is very difficult, if not virtually impossible; to be all God created us to be when we do not feel like we matter. This should not be the case with the Church. It is easier to mature in our relationship with Jesus when we experience God's love through His people. When we do not, would we say this is a problem?

A Message for a Son

One Sunday the Holy Spirit directed my attention to a young man on the other side of the sanctuary. He wanted me to give him a message. The man was alone, and appeared very troubled. When the service ended, he bolted out of the sanctuary and was across the parking lot before I caught up with him. He had to hear my high heels clacking on the pavement behind him.

He did not know I was going to deliver the word God gave me by any means necessary—including jumping on the windshield of his car if I had to. I said, "Excuse me. Can I talk to you for a minute?" He was not interested. I almost ran in the other direction from his vortex of anger. He was so mad; I could see it with his back turned.

Finally, he stopped, turned around, and looked at me like this better be good. I threw the message at him like a major-league pitcher. As my words caressed his face, tears started flowing and he could not stop crying. In that moment, He knew God cared. I did not know him, and he did not know me, but God knew his pain.

When he let his guard down, I jumped on him like a cat in hot pursuit of a mouse. I asked him if I could pray for him, and although he said yes, his countenance was saying everything but. We walked back inside the church and to the altar.

In faith, I laid hands on him and prayed with everything I knew. He stood there, hard and bitter, as I warred for his soul. Eventually, the spirit of anger tormenting him broke, and the yoke of bondage was chiseled away.

He cried harder than any man I have ever seen cry. I grabbed him in my arms, and I held him as if I was his momma, snot and all. Right then, it did not matter, I was my brother's keeper, and by the time it was over, He was free. The Kingdom had come to Earth.

God used me, because I made myself available, and He wants to use you in the same way. We are the hands, feet, and mouthpieces of the only living God. Nobody on the planet can do what we, as empowered and equipped disciples, can do.

Unbeknownst to me, the man was hurt, sad, lonely, and mad. He came to church contemplating it would be his last Sunday, and he was not coming back. He also told me afterward if anybody rubbed him the wrong way, it could be bad news. It was not an understatement when I said he was angry.

He is not the only person hurting who comes on Sunday morning and does not know what to do. Are we helping them? Not as many as we should, and that is a problem for sure.

It is vital for the family of God to treasure the ministry of one. All of Heaven rejoices over one lost soul being saved (Luke 15:10). Should we do any less once they are saved? Jesus died for the one. He died for Neicey. He died for the man I chased in the parking lot, and He died for you and me. How many ones are there sitting plastered to the pews and outside the doors of the church because we will not get off the pew? Is that a problem?

People are showing up on Sunday morning desperate for help. Do we see them? If we needed help on Sunday would we know what to do, who to ask, or how to get it, at our churches? Is the church conducive to people who do not fit into the regular Sunday routine?

The Ministry of Grace in the Five-Fold

Our greatest asset to maturing the Body of Christ is what we neglect most, the five-fold ministry of the Apostle, Prophet, Evangelist, Pastor, and Teacher, mentioned in Ephesians 4. The Scripture says it takes these five offices to grow us up. Read it for yourself. If we are to be effective, we must mature.

If we deny any of the offices in Ephesians, the Body of Christ will be compromised and the evidence of that truth is all around us. We need the anointing of the apostle to establish, plant, and lead the people. They are the ones who will give us the strategy to be victorious. Without them in position, we will not find our way out of a paper bag, let alone overcome the challenges we face.

We must encourage each other to do what Scripture says should be desired above all things, which is to prophesy (1 Corinthians 14:1). Somebody needs to speak life to the dead bones in these pews, and shine vision into the hearts of a hopeless people.

The Prophets must prophesy. There is major cause for concern when there is an absence of edification, exhortation, and the comforting of God's people. A number of times a prophetic word saved me from losing my dignified mind. Literally, how can we see without the prophets?

Surely the Lord God does nothing, unless He reveals His secret to His servants the prophets (Amos 3:7)

When Pastors are left warming the pews instead of released and empowered to shepherd the sheep, the price we pay is an undernourished, starving, and weak flock. Why are we ignoring those with a hunger in their hearts to Pastor, which is to nurture and guide His followers? Equipping is simple if we do it like Jesus did…save them, train them, and then send them out two by two.

Most Christians are unskilled on the most fundamental aspect of their faith, which is telling people about Jesus. Having the tools to evangelize is critical. Everyone with the Evangelist mantle should be undergirded and financed, because they have the anointing to compel the lost to come in. These highways and byways are waiting.

It is crucial that we not pedal a perverted evangelism to a dying and lost people, which does nothing more than repel them to the gospel—instead of compelling them to Christ. That is what happens to evangelists when they are not discipled.

Of the five offices, the teacher probably gets the least fanfare. Clearly, without them everything else is in vain. Christians do not learn because they confess Christ. This deficiency is having an alarming impact on our family. We have to shift our focus from investing in buildings to equipping people.

It is important to know, if our churches are failing at the things I mentioned, we still have a responsibility to fulfill our destinies. Unfortunately, that was something Neicey did not know. The deficit of the Church does not have to be our demise.

God has given us everything we need in His Word and through His Spirit to be victorious. Do not think He did not know some of us would have to overcome the power of that pew and His people! He also knew some of us would be led by spiritual leaders who have never become true sons. Is that your problem?

More Than A Number
Wherever Neicey went to church, people did not really know her. She was there and then she was gone. Her routine was not by choice. She spent as much time in the hospital, as she did in the pew.

We have to change the tune of our religious chant from "thanks for coming" to "we care you're here," and then we have to show it. The world teaches us to stay out of folks business, but in the Kingdom of God, we are our brother's keeper. If we are not, we should be. Galatians 6:2 says, *"Bear one another's burdens, and so fulfill the law of Christ."*

It hurts God's heart when His children have the experience of not being cared for. This is fundamental to His Kingdom on Earth. He said, *"By this all will know that you are My disciples, if you have love for one another* (John 13:35)."But, there is yet a greater issue looming in the distance.

Hear ye. Hear ye. No matter what we have experienced in our lives or in the church, we do matter. Do not believe the lie that nobody cares. We can foster an atmosphere of caring through our own behavior. Once people know they matter, then we can build a strong foundation to circumvent the plan of the enemy. Until then we have a problem.

Neicey's story is all too common, and so is mine. She was part of the Church Goers and Pew Warmers Club. I was too. Those are the people who have not been courted off the pew and into the Promise.

My story was a little different. I was fully engaged in our church, its activities, and in giving and supporting. They kept us busy. I wore out the pews
in a completely different way than Neicey. But, at the end of the day, it was all
the same.

Neicey was not growing, and neither was I in the areas that really mat-
tered. Busy just looks better. Both situations are born out of ignorance to what
is important for us as Believers.

We can sing, shout, and pray our way into a coma, and still miss the mark.
What matters is not our attendance on Sunday, our seminary degrees, or our
titles. If we go to church, but are not doing or being equipped to do what Jesus
did—we are missing the point. We are to share the Good News, heal the sick,
cast out demons, and of course, raise the dead when appropriate. We can chalk
this up to our biggest problem.

Finally, no matter what problems we encounter, we must remember this:
"*Many are the afflictions of the righteous, but the Lord delivers him out of
them all (Psalm 34:19).* "Some of our challenges will be inside the Church and
others will not. In either case, He is going to work it in our favor if we stay
humble, walk in the Fruit of the Spirit, and love unconditionally. The sooner
you we see every problem as an opportunity to learn and grow, we will learn
to appreciate the stepping-stones to our destinies.

The thief does not come except to steal, and to kill, and to destroy
(John 10:10)

Section II

The Plot
Know the Plan of the Enemy to Destroy Your Destiny

THE PLOT
The Enemy Wants You To Fail

Like millions of Church Goers, I spent decades showing up on Sunday mornings knowing I had fallen from grace a long time ago. Who was I fooling? Once I left church, I went back to my weekly routine of a life absent of God, until I needed something.

Some Christians believe that the redundant ritual of occupying the pew is equivalent to righteousness and having a relationship with Jesus Christ. This grand deception is peddled to the masses and we are drinking the Kool-Aid by the gallons. The enemy is laughing at our ignorance and he is counting on us to stay sedated by the routine.

Who does not take pride in the fact that they go to Church? Neicey and I both did. It does not matter that we do not take anyone with us, or that we play no active role in the building up of God's Kingdom. Some of us even leave people (family, friends, and guests) at home while we go give glory to the Creator.

The truth is there are no points for making it to the pew on Sunday. Some people think it is a glorious accomplishment that makes all of Heaven rejoice—which actually happens when someone repents (Luke 15:7). The rewards begin when we get off the pew and do what Jesus told us to do. Actually, what is the difference between our church-going lives and the lives of people we know who do not go to church?

Somehow, many born-again believers get the impression that the standard for being a good Christian is defined by one who goes to church? It is not true, but people live as if it is. This line of thinking is evidence of a demonic conspiracy manipulating our thoughts. News flash, there will be people in Heaven who have never graced a pew.

The enemy goes to church when the doors open and what does that mean? Nothing! He laughs, because through our repetitive generational roots, we have inadvertently reduced the birth, death, and resurrection of Jesus Christ—who came from Heaven, walked on Earth, was betrayed by one of His disciples, persecuted by the Jews, and crucified by the Romans—to us becoming professional Church Goers and Pew Warmers.

The distance between Church Going and becoming a Disciple is muddled with land minds, loopholes, and an elaborate network of demons—each with an assignment, which includes keeping us condemned to the pew.

Satan's ultimate plan is to make sure we accompany him in the eternal fires of Hell. He wants to reserve a front-row seat next to him for anyone who does not wake up and realize the snare they are caught in.

It is frightening to think how I risked my divine inheritance. Nothing I was doing was worth spending eternity separated from God. If I had to tell the truth, and nothing but the truth so help me God, I knew more was required of me then just sitting in the pew.

As long as we sit there, doing nothing, and denying the truth, we are his victims. Then he has us right where he wants us. Do not think for one minute we can give the enemy a foot, and he will not try to take our lives.

The family of God is engaged in an epic spiritual battle that is fiercely raging on every continent. We are either advancing the plan of God or helping the enemy advance his. There is no neutral territory. The casualties are massive, and once we are dead, there are no do-overs. One World Missions reports that 66,000 people die a day having no access to the gospel.[3] Jesus died so no one would be lost (2 Peter 3:9). How many of them did we know?

We, the Beloved ones of Yeshua, are in the center of the battle whether we like it or not. Ignorance of the conflict does not absolve one from the consequences. The enemy does not care if we are passive participants. Actually, he would prefer we stay ignorant to his methods and oblivious to his schemes. It makes it much easier for him to circumvent God's plan, destroy our destinies, and/or try to completely annihilate us.

In this war, the enemy does not play fair. There are no rulebooks that he must abide by and no referees. He has no mercy on his victims—and he plays for keeps. This is not a game. There is not a United Nations for this war that governs peacekeeping logistics.

He has a job to do, and a limited amount of time to get it done, so he does not procrastinate. He is aggressively engaged in accomplishing his goals and we should be too. There are many tactics the enemy deploys to harm us, and he has tremendous support to do it. His methods are malicious, highly deceptive, and outright destructive.

He is serious, focused, and organized. This is not about giving him accolades. It is important for us to know our adversary is very equipped and highly skilled. We are stronger and more powerful if we have the right tools, and we know how to use them.

He is counting on us to disobey God and yield to his scams. The enemy knows there is no middle ground even if we do not. We are either hot or cold, and if we are lukewarm, God said, "*I will spew you out of My mouth* (Revelation 3:16)."

The enemy nurtures his schemes when we are unaware of his deceptive measures and ignorant of the Word of God. He plants morsels of untruths and then he waters them. Once we accept the lies as truth, he's got us, *bam*! Have we ever wondered how his lies get in? Here are a few ways to equip us, but there are many:

- Lies can come directly from the enemy
  - They enter in the form of thoughts he sends directly into our minds (Ephesians 6:16)
  - He wants us to own them, but they are not ours
  - We have to take those thoughts captive so they do not take root (2 Corinthians 10:5)
- Some lies come through the iniquity of our parents and/or our ancestors
  - We had nothing to do with it
  - It is genetically in our bloodstreams
  - "The apple does not fall far from the tree"
  - Something from our parents is being identified in us
- Others come from having sex with someone we are not married to
  - Intercourse opens the door for transfer spirits
  - Now we know some of our drama is not ours, it belongs to someone else
- Self-delusion is probably at the top of the list
  - Often, churchgoers do not want to admit that they are falling short
  - They prefer to stay in denial
- Fear always opens the door for the enemy because God did not give us a spirit of fear (2 Timothy 1:7)

His attacks start long before you can even talk. Frank and Ida Mae Hammond said in *A Manual for Children's Deliverance*, "It is our conviction that as soon as a child is conceived, the devil forms a plot and a plan to capture and destroy his life." The innocence of a baby, or a child, is no deterrent for the enemy's brutality. He is systematic. He is strategic and he is vicious. As parents, it is our responsibility to protect our children from the darts of the enemy.

It is easy to believe his lies when we do not know the Word, which is why we have to study, study, study. Since the enemy is the Father of lies, he is counting on our spiritual ignorance to fertilize his plan. It says it in John 8:44,"*He was a murderer from the beginning, and does not stand in the truth, because there is no truth in him. When he speaks a lie, he speaks from his own resources, for he is a liar and the father of it.*" He sets out to seed the soil of our minds with little foxes, because the little foxes spoil the vine (Song of Solomon 2:15).

When the plot of the enemy is in full swing, we do not usually know it. He slowly moves us farther away from our destinies. He wants to erode anything Christlike in us. His demonic manure is excreted in our minds, down to our hearts, and out our mouths. It is as foul as it sounds, and eventually we become contaminated vessels.

At some point, if we do not run into a pair of pruning shears, we are going to be in serious trouble. The Scriptures say in John 15:2,"*Every branch in Me that does not bear fruit He takes away; and every branch that bears fruit He prunes, that it may bear more fruit.*" People caught in the snare of the enemy have a difficult time growing spiritually. Have we grown? How would we know? When it comes to a relationship with Christ, anything that is not growing is going to be cut down, thrown into the fire, and burned (John 15:6).

The enemy uses a host of things to destroy our destinies; denial is just the beginning. He will vex our emotions and mental capacities. He wants us paralyzed and unable to get up off that pew.

His favorite trick is to burden us with is un-forgiveness, bad feelings toward others, and bitterness. Or he sets us up to dishonor our parents and bring a curse on ourselves. He makes sure women disrespect their husbands and husbands are unloving toward their wives, because he knows God prohibits both.

Finally, if none of these work, he will attack our bodies with sickness and disease. Do not underestimate him. If he can take our lives, he will, just read the book of Job in the Bible. The enemy's schemes are treacherous, and he does not care about consequences.

The Plot: Jesus Is Not The Messiah

Foremost, the enemy does not want us to believe Jesus is the Messiah, the Son of God, Savior of the World, or that He really exists. This reality is true to the tune of almost four billion people, on the planet, who are unbelievers.[4] He is exceptionally clever at convincing people to reject their ticket to eternal life.

The Plot: We Do Not Need the Baptism of the Holy Spirit

Another aspect of his plot is to make sure we do not pursue being filled with the Holy Spirit. He knows the Holy Spirit will guide us into all truth and expose his lies. He also knows without the Holy Spirit we lack the power necessary to overcome him.

If we are not baptized in the Spirit, it cannot help us and the enemy knows this. He wants us to be satisfied with water baptism only because it alone it is not enough. Some of the biggest splits in Christian church history were over Holy Spirit related matters and the enemy is behind it.

The Plot: The Enemy Is Not Real

His first line of defense is to convince us, through deception, he does not exist. If we do not believe he is real, then we are already doomed. As long as we deny his existence, then we are NO threat to his Kingdom.

There was a time in my life when my choices convinced me the devil was not real. Yes, we can shift from belief to unbelief. I asked God how was that possible. He told me the eyes of my understanding began to darken as I opened my heart to the ways of the world (Ephesians 4:18-19)

Here are a few of the mistakes I made giving the enemy direct access:

- Saying I was a Christian, but not living like one.
- Seeking my daily horoscope for insight about my life (which is practicing witchcraft)
- Unknowingly opening the door to seducing spirits through hypnosis (What was I thinking?)
- Practicing New Age activities

Nothing I mentioned is an innocent gesture as so many Christians often think. Being spiritually naïve made me vulnerable for the enemy to have his way with me, and he did.

Here is a personal example of how easy it is for the enemy to distort the truth and feed us deception like it is our favorite food. Because I was the oldest girl in a single-female headed household, I got the brunt of the work, including taking care of my siblings. At least it felt that way to me.

The pressure to help my mother care for her house was too much, but I did not know how to communicate that when I was ten. By the time I was eighteen, all I wanted was to be alone. The thought of having children was far from my mind. I could not wait *not* to be responsible for someone else. Little did I know the enemy was stirring his pot for my demise.

In order to understand the plot, we have to understand God's plan. His core plan for woman is to be fruitful and multiply. In my childbearing years, the only thing I wanted to multiply was time by myself. My mind was already being fashioned against the things of God.

It was never God's plan for children to be reared by single parents. Being overworked, underpaid, and totally stressed out trying to make ends meet was not His intention for anyone. However, it was the reality for my mom.

The enemy continued to cultivate his vicious scheme and I was being demonically manipulated without me knowing it. The very reason I was created, as a woman, was being sabotaged. He progressively dismantled my creation destiny by stealing the children from my womb, and he succeeded, because I did not know the truth.

When the Scripture said, "My people perish for a lack of knowledge" (Hosea 4:6) we should know a whole lot dies before we expire. Unless I am selected for supernatural conception, there will be no children coming from this womb. Once I realized the truth, it broke my heart. Then the Word gave me comfort and assurance.

So I will restore to you the years that the swarming locust has eaten,
the crawling locust, the consuming locust, and the chewing locust
(Joel 2:25)

As the eyes of our understanding are opened, we too might recognize the enemies' scheme is in operation in our lives. Does anything come to mind? We can be assured God has a plan and He made us a promise that He would complete what He started (Philippians 1:6).

For they intended evil against You; They devised a plot which they are not
able to perform (Psalm 21:11)

There is no way we can perceive all the plots of the enemy, but now some of it—is exposed.

Not everyone who says to Me, 'Lord, Lord,' shall enter the kingdom of heaven, but he who does the will of My Father in heaven. Many will say to Me in that day, 'Lord, Lord, have we not prophesied in Your name, cast out demons in Your name, and done many wonders in Your name? And then I will declare to them, 'I never knew you; depart from Me, you who practice lawlessness' (Matthew 7:21-23)

Section III

The Players
Know the Key Players So You
Recognize the Truth Or A Deception

THE PLAYERS

When we are thoroughly versed on the role and responsibilities of the key players in the Kingdom, we can have the upper hand. I am specifically talking about the individual person, the Christian, the Church, God, Jesus, the Holy Spirit, the Bible, the Kingdom of God, the World, and the Enemy.

Without basic knowledge of what I call the Big Ten it is impossible to decipher when someone or something in the core regime is perverted. Knowing the truth makes it easier to see the deception. This section will build our ability to identify both the real and the counterfeit.

Have you seen the movie or read the novel *Left Behind* written by Tim LaHaye and Jerry B. Jenkins? It highlights the second coming of Christ and those who are left behind because they did not believe (Matthew 24:40-44). The focus is on the characters that pretend to be Christian or never converted.

The movie shows the chaos and fear that will erupt once God's chosen people are removed from the Earth. They will be snatched up with Jesus at His glorious Second Coming. The most intriguing character in the movie for me was the pastor who was left behind. He was impersonating a Christian. How many in his flock do you think knew he was a tare (Matthew 13:24-30)?

The Pastor was in utter disbelief when he realized what he was preaching was real. If an infidel is touting the gospel, it does not make it less true. There are those of us who plant and others water, but it is the Lord God on high who makes it grow (1 Corinthians 3:6).

Now, if you have a biblical understanding of the Kingdom, and those in it, you will be less likely to have misinformed expectations. Also, you will not be so easily offended and unnecessarily wounded.

Here are some questions to ponder that will help you focus your learning about the key players. Try to answer the questions if you can. Or, discuss them with another person. You might be surprised by what you already know.

- Do you know for sure you are born-again? How?
- How do you know if you are on the right track or not, in the maturing of your faith?
- Can you discern good and evil?
- Are you meeting the standards of being a true Christian?
- How would you know if you were involved in a counterfeit move of the Holy Spirit?
- What is the difference between God, Jesus, and the Holy Spirit?

- Do you know when you or someone else is being used by the enemy?

As you mature in your relationship with Jesus you should be able to answer these questions. Showing up on Sunday, sitting in a pew, is not necessarily going to get you the answers. You have to study, but not to be religious. Nobody wants to be beat over the head with the Word of God, and trust me I have been.

Let It Go
It is highly probable you or someone you know has been hurt by one or several of the key players. On their behalf would you please release them from their offense and accept this apology as a proxy gesture?

I am sorry for the hurt you experienced, and how it has affected your life. You may have been ostracized, treated unfairly, ignored, or perhaps emotionally, verbally or even physically abused, neglected, minimized and/or rejected. Please forgive me if I forgot anything. I tried to include some of the things that have happened to me, knowing they have happened to others.

Let me caution you, you have to forgive and release them, in order to be forgiven. Of course, sooner is better than later. This is the path to healing, and your own inner revival!

But I say to you, love your enemies, bless those who curse you, do good to those who hate you, and pray for those who spitefully use you and persecute you (Matthew 5:44).

THE PLAYERS: YOU

The Human Being

THE TRUTH: *For all have sinned and fall short of the glory of God (Romans 3:23)*
THE DECEPTION: You do not have to be born again

Behold, I stand at the door and knock. If anyone hears My voice and opens
the door, I will come in to him and dine with him, and he with Me
(Revelation 3:20)

What comes to mind when you ponder we are created in the image of God? The one who hung the stars and the moon—He who holds back the seas from flooding the earth. The voice who said in the beginning, "Let there be light.", and there was. Imagine you have the same capacity to speak things into existence as a Believer. Now, that is outrageously amazing!

The first human created was Adam, a man. Adam made the mistake of disobeying God, and it caused all of humanity to be born into sin, which separates us from God.

If we say that we have no sin, we deceive ourselves, and the truth is not in us.
If we confess our sins, He is faithful and just to forgive us our sins
and to cleanse us from all unrighteousness (1 John 1:8-9)

There is nothing else created in the Heavens or on the Earth in the image of God other than human beings. We are unique, extraordinary, and fearfully and wonderfully made (Psalm 139:14).What is required of our lives can be understood in why and who created us (Isaiah 43:7). We can always go to the Scriptures to find the answers to anything we want to know.

So God created man in His own image; in the image of God He created him;
male and female He created them. Then God blessed them, and God said to
them, "Be fruitful and multiply; fill the earth and subdue it; have dominion
over the fish of the sea, over the birds of the air, and over every living thing
that moves on the earth" (Genesis 1:27-28)

We exist for God's glory…and to have dominion. He made us the head and not the tail (Deuteronomy 28:13). We are more than a conqueror (Romans 8:37). If we are not, we should be.

Every person on the planet needs a savior, and each one of us has to make a conscious choice to be reconciled back to God and reconnected to His family.

This includes the Jews and Gentiles. The Republicans and Democrats, rich and the poor, the intellectuals, and the uneducated. The famous and the infamous too. No exceptions.

What are the adjectives that describe why you need a Savior?

_____

Write the words that describe YOU here ↑

There are many people, including Believers, who think being a good person is enough. Brace yourself. You might want to sit down. This could be a shock to your system. It is not. In the sight of God, none are good.

> *So Jesus said to him, "Why do you call Me good?*
> *No one is good but One, that is, God (Luke 18:19)*

How exactly does one define a good person anyway, and whose criteria are we using? Can we see the motives of a person's heart? The Bible says all our righteousness is as filthy rags (Isaiah 64:6). The *Literal Translation New King James Bible* says it like this, *"But we are all as the unclean thing, and all our righteousnesses are as a menstruation cloth."* Simply put, our best is really, really gross.

Scripture goes on to say our hearts are also pitiful. *"The heart is deceitful above all things, and desperately wicked; Who can know it (Jeremiah 17:9)?"* We think we are more than we are when we believe we are good outside of God. It is the nature of the beast called *self*.

We cannot do anything on our own. Many of us have tried, and I too am guilty. Our hearts beat because God allows them to. It is His breath, the *ruach*, that He breathes everyday into our nostrils. We are only one breath away from meeting our Maker.

Many people ignore that after this life is eternity, the place where forever has no end. We can easily accept deception when we refuse to acknowledge we have a natural and spiritual body (1 Corinthians 15:44).

Now may the God of peace Himself sanctify you completely; and may your whole spirit, soul, and body be preserved blameless at the coming of our Lord Jesus Christ (1 Thessalonians 5:23)

The Spirit

We all have a spirit, a body, and a soul. Our spirits are the part that must be regenerated, because through sin—which we were born into—it was separated from the Creator. The only way to be reconciled to God is to be born again. We can only be reconnected to God through our spirits. No other avenue will work.

The Body

Our bodies are called *the flesh*. They will eventually die and to the disappointment of the many, who believe otherwise, we will **NOT** be reincarnated.

For out of it you were taken; For dust you *are*,
And to dust you shall return (Genesis 3:19)

The Soul

The soul is where our mind, will, and emotions originate. This area is seriously neglected by the Body of Christ. The soul is where the emotional wounds driving bad behavior are hidden. People get a sour taste in their mouth about Christianity because they are watching us live out of our souls. The Father provides a strategy for the salvation of the soul. Check this out:

Therefore lay aside all filthiness and overflow of wickedness, and receive with meekness the implanted word, which is able to save your souls (James 1:21)

The Scripture also says,

For what will it profit a man if he gains the whole world, and loses his own soul (Mark 8:36)

To get our souls saved, we have to do something. When it comes to the salvation of our spirits, we only have to believe. First Fruits Ministry put it like this, *"The difference between spirit salvation and soul salvation is the difference between grace and works. The spirit is saved by faith in Jesus Christ, while the soul is saved by faithfulness to Jesus Christ. Soul salvation does not determine whether a person enters heaven, but it does determine his reward in heaven."*[5]

Each one's work will become clear; for the Day will declare it, because it will be revealed by fire; and the fire will test each one's work, of what sort it is. If anyone's work which he has built on it endures, he will receive a reward. If anyone's work is burned, he will suffer loss; but he himself will be saved (1 Corinthians 3:13-15)

In order to come from under the deceptive lies of the enemy, we have to renew our minds. Renewal can only happen with the Word of God. The Word is like spiritual Tide. It can clean even the toughest stains of darkness.

And do not be conformed to this world, but be transformed by the renewing of your mind, that you may prove what is that good and acceptable and perfect will of God (Romans 12:2)

DISCIPLE ME NOW: Learn – Grow- Practice - Go
The Truth
- We are sinners; if we do not believe this, we are deceived (1 John 1:8)
- It is easy to become a born-again Christian (Romans 10:9)
- Once a person confesses their sins, God will forgive them and cleanse them from all unrighteousness (1 John 1:9)
- We are either children of God or children of the devil; there is no in-between (1 John 3:10)
- Our names must be written in the Book of Life: *And anyone not found written in the Book of Life was cast into the lake of fire (Revelation 20:15)*

- If we are not born again, we cannot comprehend spiritual things even though we try: *But the natural man does not receive the things of the Spirit of God, for they are foolishness to him; nor can he know* them, *because they are spiritually discerned (1 Corinthians 2:14)*
- The state of man before he accepts Christ is horrific: *Because you say, I am rich, have become wealthy, and have need of nothing'—and do not know that you are wretched, miserable, poor, blind, and naked (Revelation 3:17)*
- For if you live according to the flesh you will die; but if by the Spirit you put to death the deeds of the body, you will live (Romans 8:13)
- Sin costs: *For the wages of sin is death, but the gift of God is eternal life in Christ Jesus our Lord (Romans 6:23)*
- There is no excuse for not knowing God is real: *For since the creation of the world His invisible* attributes *are clearly seen, being understood by the things that are made,* even *His eternal power and Godhead, so that they are without excuse (Romans 1:20)*
- God is giving us time to choose life *(2 Peter 3:9)*
- Until we accept Jesus Christ as Lord, we are blind: *To open their eyes, in order to turn them from darkness to light, and from the power of Satan to God, that they may receive forgiveness of sins and an inheritance among those who are sanctified by faith in Me (Acts 26:18)*

The Deception
- Hell is not real—FALSE (Revelation 21:8)
- There is more than one way to Jesus—FALSE (John 14:6)
- There are no consequences if we die and we are not born again—FALSE—if we die and we are not born again, we will spend eternity separated from God (Romans 6:23)
- We have all the time in the world to get saved—FALSE—*Do not boast about tomorrow, for you do not know what a day may bring forth (Proverbs 27:1)*
- Only the bad people need Jesus—FALSE—Every person, without exception, needs Jesus as Lord and Savior
- We can work to achieve righteousness—FALSE
- We can be reincarnated—FALSE—*And as it is appointed for men to die once, but after this the judgment (Hebrews 9:27)*

THE PLAYERS: **THE WORLD**

Past, Present or Future Defined Ages and Prevailing Conditions including the Stars, Trees, People, Nations and the Evil System[6]

THE TRUTH: *Do you not know that friendship with the world is enmity with God? Whoever therefore wants to be a friend of the world makes himself an enemy of God (James 4:4)*
THE DECEPTION: The world loves you

In order to avoid becoming a victim of spiritual adultery, there is much to learn about how God wants His children to function in the world and with the world. There are five references to the world I will highlight for our mental repertoire. The systems of the world will put us in direct contradiction with the ways of God, unless we understand how to be in the world, but not of it.

Before we begin, I will be transparent about the issue I had with the pride of life, one of the five references. This area needed serious purging, and God has generously provided. My problem was covetousness, which means hungering for, desiring, craving or having my heart set on. However, not in the way you might think. I did not desire what belonged to someone else.

Most of us can understand coveting something that is not ours, but what about when it is? We can covet our own stuff and that was my problem. I was yearning for what was. Coveting was a mountain in me that needed to be moved, particularly when I thought about the life I had before Christ. This perspective may not be common, but it can be a problem nonetheless.

Often, I found myself boasting about what I had accomplished when I was in sin. The problem wasn't what I shared, it was why I was sharing. It took a long time for me to notice what I was doing and why. I wanted attention and God was training me on the focus belonging to Him. Longevity in character development is usually a sign we are not ready to face the reality of who we are and allow God to change us.

As I continued to grow in my faith, and the layers of secular conditioning got thinner, the flaws in my character became easier to see. The stronghold needed to be broken, and it took time and intentional work to overcome. First, I had to acknowledge the error of my ways.

This is how I was transformed. I had to deal with what was behind my need to flaunt my accomplishments. It was pride, which looked like me using my success to defend my honor. In either case, the response caused me to be puffed up.

Once it was revealed by the Holy Spirit and I recognized it, I was on to something. The need for attention is a byproduct of selfishness and does not line up with righteousness. My character was out of order and it had to be realigned.

We often find ourselves on these disappointing voyages of looking in the wrong places for what we need. Eventually, we figure out we are chasing unconditional love. If we do not read our Bibles, it is impossible to know. The Word told me I had a problem in this area. Our issues will not always be pointed out by a person, some things are intended to be brought to the surface through our relationship with Christ .

Deliverance ministry taught me that my need to be acknowledged was rooted in a spirit of rejection and abandonment. My initial deliverance was wonderful and then I continued doing self-deliverance, a method of healing that allowed me to target the emotional scars and wounds on my soul, at home. The damage to our souls is what causes us to be hurt, act like plum fools, embarrass ourselves and say things we often regret. I am guilty of them all.

Once I started letting the Word of God into the innermost parts of my soul, to heal what was broken, it began to change my relationships. And, boy did it feel good. We know we are being transformed from the inside out when our automatic reactions to negative things people say and do begin to subside. We are less volatile, and the little tug we feel inside when someone does something hurtful is not there anymore. We are making serious progress when we are not so easily hurt or agitated.

When we are devoted to the world, and its standards of operation, it is easy to act worldly. It means we are being unfaithful to God. Being aware of this nature in our character is vital and for our own protection. It is important to understand we cannot be loyal to both. Here is the bottom line: love for the things of the world causes our love for God to erode.

The world promotes the pursuit of knowledge and God prefers the truth. In the world, pride is an asset, but God honors humility. Secular society wants us to defend ourselves or we are considered cowards, and God said let Him fight our battles (2 Chronicles 20:15). The world wants our affection and God is a jealous God (Exodus 34:14). He will not share us with anyone or anything.

Here are the five references:

#1 The enemy is the god of this world. *In whose case the god of this world has blinded the minds of the unbelieving so that they might not see the light of the gospel of the glory of Christ, who is the image of God (2 Corinthians 4:4) NASB*

#2 There are three things in the world we should know about. *For all that is in the world—the lust of the flesh, the lust of the eyes, and the pride of life— is not of the Father but is of the world (1 John 2:16)*

The three things we will face in the world each has its own thorns and offers a unique way to sabotage our destinies. We can be fully aware of what that entails. *Because the foolishness of God is wiser than men, and the weakness of God is stronger than men (1 Corinthians 1:25)*

We can approach each category with wisdom. We must choose in which Kingdom we are going to function. We cannot have two Masters, because we will love one and hate the other (Matthew 6:24).

The Pride of Life

Meaning: The King James Version dictionary defines pride as an unhealthy desire for recognition. Inordinate self-esteem; an unreasonable conceit of one's own superiority in talents, beauty, wealth, accomplishments, rank or elevation in office, which manifests itself in lofty airs, distance, reserve, and often in contempt of others.[7]

The pride of life shows up in our conduct and consists of the deliberate pursuit of recognition, honor, and ambition. We might have noticed there is a lot of this going on in the church. We cannot control what anybody else is doing, but we can manage ourselves.

As a former pageant winner, I know firsthand what it feels like to be seduced by the praise of men. It can be difficult to get free from its clutches. God never intended for worship to be directed toward man.

Now pride is not always a bad thing, but when it is, it has a foul fragrance easy to identify. The opposite of pride is humility, which is highly sought after in the Kingdom of God. Pride and humility cannot coexist. The position of humility will take us further than any other attribute (Luke 14:7-11).

Folks do not compete to be like Mother Theresa, because who wants to strive for the low places? The epitome of humility is when Jesus surrendered His will to the will of God. He agreed to be crucified for the sins of the world. We cannot go any lower than what He did.

Lust of the Flesh
Meaning: Strong or unhealthy cravings or desire of vile affections, luxury, or of a sexual nature.

Temptations in this life are going to come. It is almost impossible to avoid, but God said He would give us a way of escape.

No temptation has overtaken you except such as is common to man; but God is faithful, who will not allow you to be tempted beyond what you are able, but with the temptation will also make the way of escape, that you may be able to bear it (1 Corinthians 10:13)

He offers supernatural loopholes for every situation we may encounter. Here is a simple one: *Therefore submit to God. Resist the devil and he will flee from you (James 4:7)*

We do not have to be a victim of our passions and lusts. The perfect example is the life of His Son, Jesus, while He was here on earth. He did not yield to the lust or the temptations of grandeur. It is possible for us to be victorious in this area as well.

For the weapons of our warfare are not carnal but mighty in God for pulling down strongholds, casting down arguments and every high thing that exalts itself against the knowledge of God, bringing every thought into captivity to the obedience of Christ (2 Corinthians 10:4-5)

Here are the works of the flesh we want to remove from our lives and avoid at all costs:

Now the works of the flesh are evident, which are: adultery, fornication, uncleanness, lewdness, idolatry, sorcery, hatred, contentions, jealousies, outbursts of wrath, selfish ambitions, dissensions, heresies, envy, murders, drunkenness, revelries, and the like (Galatians 5:19-21)

Before we go any further, let's take a moment to clean up the error of our ways. If we know we are guilty of any of these works, we can confess them to God, or to a brother or sister in Christ that we trust. Then repent from the behavior immediately and step into freedom.

Lust of the Eyes

Meaning: Unhealthy desire for what we see visually.

We can learn to manage the portals of our eye-gates. Our eyes are the doors to our hearts and thoughts. They are easily used as the vehicle to distract, deceive, and destroy if we let them. It is important to make sure every portal is purified and held shut by the blood of Jesus. The only way to prevent lust of the eyes from flourishing is to walk in the Spirit.

To covet is to desire, yearn, crave, want, long for, wish to have, hunger, or lust for. One of the Ten Commandments is we are not to covet (Exodus 20:17). List three things you are coveting. Then confess it, repent, and let go by faith.

1. _____

2._____

3._____

Coveting can be overcome when we learn to be grateful for what we have and our resources can afford. Wanting what someone else has can get us into serious trouble. As the saying goes, "The grass always looks greener on the other side," but it usually is not.

#3 We are not to be drawn away by the teachings of the world. *Beware lest anyone cheat you through philosophy and empty deceit, according to the* *tradition of men, according to the basic principles of the world, and not according to Christ (Colossians 2:8)*

We have to be very careful with the things offered by the world. When we evaluate what is being taught, does it lead us back to Christ, or away from Him? Always keep that in mind.

#4 If we trust God, and not man, we will always come out on top. *But God has chosen the foolish things of the world to put to shame the wise, and God has chosen the weak things of the world to put to shame the things which are mighty (1 Corinthians 1:27)*

There is nothing more amazing than to see God take a situation you processed through your natural intellect, and then He works it out in His wisdom. He always does it better. You never look as good as when God prepares a table for you in the presence of your enemies. Glory to God, I feel a shout coming!

#5 One of the most important Scriptures to learn: *And do not be conformed to this world, but be transformed by the renewing of your mind, that you may prove what is that good and acceptable and perfect will of God (Romans 12:2)*

Progressive development in our salvation hinges on us being able to renew our minds, especially from the world's conditioning. If we want to change anything, we have to change the way we think first. Speakers and authors make millions telling people how they should think.

The hardest part of changing our minds—is doing it. Nike paid a lot of money to teach the world…*just do it!* We can renew our mind by coming into a greater relationship with Him and His Word.

To renew our minds is the equivalent of renovating a home. If we want to bring an old dilapidated house up to date, we have to give it a major overhaul. We might need to remove all the old stuff, including the carpet, the old wooden floors, and the furniture that is outdated. In our minds, the old ways of thinking have to be tossed.

Then we will perhaps tear down a few walls to reconfigure the house. We call those strongholds in the mind. They are stubborn perspectives, generational inheritances, and/or cultural beliefs we have subscribed to, been conditioned by, or socialized into.

For sure the old fixtures will be swapped out for more modern ones. Our thinking has to be updated from what we think to what God thinks. Then there are those things that only need to be tweaked and some that can be refurbished. The renewing of our minds works the same way.

Since getting saved, my thinking has shifted many times. My thoughts are continually coming into alignment with Scripture. A carnal mindset is not complimentary to the Spirit. Being double-minded makes one unstable in all his ways and is the quickest way to become SMI (seriously mentally ill).

One of my most memorable transformations happened when I realized I could not change anyone. That was hard for me, because I spent years traveling around the country doing transformational workshops with thousands of people. I was there to help them change. What I know now is I gave them a false hope.

Motivational speakers are invested in saying that lives are changed because of what they say or offer in their programs or seminars. We cannot change anyone, and the sooner I got that revelation, the better my life was. Eventually, rhetoric will fail us all.

In deliverance ministry, week after week, we looked at people who were suffering because they will not renew their minds. It pained me terribly because I could relate. I wanted people in my family to stop drinking or doing drugs, and to stop tripping with their drama. My attempts to fix people only failed, and often my efforts to change them backfired. Eventually, I came to the conclusion it was only me that I could change, and I could stay busy with that for a lifetime.

What we think about—or allow into our thoughts—are important, because it helps or hurts our walk with God. We have to block much of the stuff from the world. The Bible says this, *"Finally, brethren, whatever things are true, whatever things are noble, whatever things are just, whatever things are pure, whatever things are lovely, whatever things are of good report, if there is any virtue and if there is anything praiseworthy—meditate on these things (Philippians 4:8).* We learn a lot of things, but has anyone taught us how to think?

Just in case the thought came up, this is not about positive thinking. We can think positive all day, in everything we do, about everyone we encounter, and it can have nothing to do with Christ. This is called vain philosophies, and the world is full of it. The renewing is an alignment that comes from dismissing that which does not line up with His Word and embracing what does.

DISCIPLE ME NOW: Learn – Grow – Practice - Go

The Truth About Pride

- *A man's pride will bring him low, but the humble in spirit will retain honor (Proverbs 29:23)*
- *Pride goes before destruction, and a haughty spirit before a fall (Proverbs 16:18)*
- *Let another man praise you, and not your own mouth; a stranger, and not your own lips (Proverbs 27:2)*
- *God resists the proud, but gives grace to the humble (James 4:6)*
- *Do you see a man who is wise in his own eyes? There is more hope for a fool than for him (Proverbs 26:12)*
- *Thus says the Lord: "Let not the wise man glory in his might, let not the mighty man glory in his might, let not the rich man glory in his riches (Jeremiah 9:23)*
- *Let nothing be done through selfish ambition or conceit, but in lowliness of mind let each esteem others better than himself (Philippians 2:3)*
- *The fear of the Lord is to hate evil; Pride and arrogance and the evil way and the perverse mouth I hate (Proverbs 8:13)*
- *For I say, through the grace given to me, to everyone who is among you, not to think of himself more highly than he ought to think, but to think soberly (Romans 12:3)*
- *Better to be of a humble spirit with the lowly, than to divide the spoil with the proud (Proverbs 16:19)*

The Truth About Lust

- *But each one is tempted when he is drawn away by his own desires and enticed. Then, when desire has conceived, it gives birth to sin; and sin, when it is full-grown, brings forth death (James 1:14-15)*
- *Beloved, I beg you as sojourners and pilgrims, abstain from fleshly lusts which war against the soul (1 Peter 2:11)*

- *So then, those who are in the flesh cannot please God (Romans 8:8)*
- *And He said, "What comes out of a man, that defiles a man. For from within, out of the heart of men, proceed evil thoughts, adulteries, fornications, murders, thefts, covetousness, wickedness, deceit, lewdness, an evil eye, blasphemy, pride, foolishness. All these evil things come from within and defile a man" (Mark 7:20-23)*
- *I say then: Walk in the Spirit, and you shall not fulfill the lust of the flesh (Galatians 5:16)*
- *For if you live according to the flesh you will die, but if by the Spirit you put to death the deeds of the body, you will live (Romans 8:13)*
- *Flee sexual immorality. Every sin that a man does is outside the body, but he who commits sexual immorality sins against his own body (1 Corinthians 6:18)*
- *Therefore do not let sin reign in your mortal body, that you should obey it in its lusts. And do not present your members as instruments of unrighteousness to sin, but present yourselves to God as being alive from the dead, and your members as instruments of righteousness to God (Romans 6:12-13)*
- *That which is born of the flesh is flesh, and that which is born of the Spirit is spirit (John 3:6)*
- *Watch and pray, lest you enter into temptation. The spirit indeed is willing, but the flesh is weak (Matthew 26:41)*
- *For he who sows to his flesh will of the flesh reap corruption, but he who sows to the Spirit will of the Spirit reap everlasting life (Galatians 6:8)*

The Deception
- *This world will exist forever—FALSE—And the world is passing away, and the lust of it; but he who does the will of God abides forever (1 John 2:17)*
- *You can love the world. FALSE Do not love the world or the things in the world. If anyone loves the world, the love of the Father is not in him (1 John 2:15)*

THE PLAYERS: THE ENEMY

Spiritual Adversary

THE TRUTH: The devil is real, and he is not a fictional character. *The thief does not come except to steal, and to kill, and to destroy (John 10:10)*
THE DECEPTION: The devil is not real, and he does not exist

If we have a basic understanding of the enemy and how he operates, we will be better positioned to avoid and/or dismantle his plan to destroy us. It takes a lot less energy to battle the enemy from an offensive position VS defensive.

After reading a nationwide study by the Barna group titled, "Most Christians Do Not Believe that Satan or the Holy Spirit Exists" I was nothing short of flabbergasted. I knew it was true, but I did not know it was that bad. If we are Christians, we must line up with the basic tenants of our own faith, and these two are at the top of the list. Satan and the Holy Spirit are real.

How can we believe in God, and not His enemy? Everyone in the genealogy of Jesus Christ has an enemy. Who does not have enemies anyway? The devil, who is the enemy, is a disturbing character, and all it takes is one encounter to be convinced of his existence. When we hear people talking about having nightmares or seeing ghost, most likely they have had a run-in with the enemy. Now, that is not the case all the time.

The Enemy Is Real
There was a time when I believed the devil was not real, just like many do. Once the eyes of my understanding were opened, I learned how that came to be.

Everything started to change when I unconsciously decided to lean away from my childhood faith. It would be safe to say during the time I did not believe the enemy existed, I also was not in alignment with my beliefs. Unbelief moved in so subtly I did not notice when it started.

As I got older, I began to explore the world around me, and indulge in the diversity of faith-like paths that satisfied my spiritual hunger. What harm can there be in the indulgence of the self, the vibes of enlightenment or dabbling in New Age? Actually, it can be tragic.

IGNORANCE is the devil's delicacy. This is the easiest way for him to circumvent God's plan in Believers. But it does not have to be a stage-four terminal diagnosis. We can overcome and conquer all of his traps if we raise our game.

The Enemy's kryptonite is when we study and apply the Word of God. His days of controlling our lives are numbered the minute we start. But don't be surprised because he might very well turn up the heat as an attempt to turn us back to our old ways.

Things To Know About the Enemy
- He is a fallen angel and was perfect in beauty (Ezekiel 28:12)
- Satan is a spirit, not flesh and blood
- He is the embodiment of evil
- He is diabolical
- He is powerful and should be considered a formidable foe
- He is the Prince of the air and the god of the earth (Ephesians 2:2)
- He is a liar and the Father of lies (John 8:44)
- He knows God and Scripture better than we ever will
- He is not more powerful than God or the Holy Spirit inside of Believers (1John 4:4)
- We have authority over the devil and his demons, if we use it
- He is a master at manipulating our thoughts
- He is empowered through the lies and deception that we come into agreement with
- His name in Greek is *diabolos*, which means *accuser* or *slander* (Revelation 12:10)
- He wants to devour us (1 Peter 5:8)
- He can be defeated

He disguises himself as an angel of light (2 Corinthians 11:14). The devil is part of the unseen realm, although he has a way of making himself known. If we cannot see, or do not know the devil is real, then our eyes are either blinded to the Kingdom of Darkness, or we know—but we are denying the truth. In either case, as a Christian, we have a problem.

Unbelief will blind our spiritual sight. Doubt will also close our eyes as well. The enemy only has the capacity to blind us because we choose to not believe. Believe what? We choose not to believe in Jesus Christ. In 2 Corinthians 3:16 it reveals the veil of blindness is removed when one turns to Christ.

One of the worst things I have experienced was getting attacked by demons while I was sleeping. The first time it happened they were smothering me in my sleep. I could not fight back, because I felt paralyzed. In psychiatry this is called sleep paralysis.

My breath was being siphoned so I could not scream either. The feeling of being suffocated was awful. It is hard to fight what we cannot see. Every few seconds I would come to a level of semi-consciousness, and it would stop. Then I would fall back into a deep sleep, and it would happen again. There are no words to describe the horror I felt.

Finally, I broke free. It felt as if I had been waging war for hours. I woke up in a panic, hysterical and upset, because I had been physically touched by an evil spirit. Somehow during the ordeal I had the wherewithal to call on the name of Jesus, and they stopped immediately.

Before that happened to me, I had only heard a few stories of such a thing. Mostly, what I knew about the devil I had seen on television, and like many of you think now, it did not seem real. Who would believe this stuff really happens? Do people actually get thrown across rooms or levitate like in the movies? The answer is *yes*, and sometimes much worse.

Actually, it is happening all day, every day, somewhere and to someone. Women, men, and children are being assaulted by demons. I know this from experience. Fortunately for me, I was able to take authority, by calling on the name of Jesus, before a spirit succeeded at trying to sexually assault me. But, many people have not been as fortunate.

Can demonic spirits choke us until we cannot breathe? Yes, they did it to me. Spiritually demonic mischief happens to people in our families, who we fellowship with, and folks we work with as well. For some of us, our children are victims of demons, or our spouses and siblings; we just do not know it.

This might be hard to believe, but we can ask one of these two questions— to any ten people we know—and there is a 100% chance at least one of them will answer *yes*. First question: *Have you ever felt like you were attacked, suffocated, or touched by something dark or demonic while you were asleep?* Second question: *Have you ever seen, felt, or heard something you knew was from the dark side of the spirit world?*

A lot of Christians are being tormented by demons, and they are too afraid to tell anyone. They know what is happening to them is real, but it is difficult to explain. Others have been convinced they are crazy, and the dark shadows they see are imaginary, or the voices they hear are only in their head.

Demonic oppression, torture, and seduction is as real as our breath. We cannot see it, but we know it is there. Spirits are rarely visible to the natural eye, but our discernment can tell us when they are in the room. Some people can see them with their natural eye.

In Scriptures, it says deliverance is the children's bread. Jesus is telling us being delivered from bad spirits is our inheritance. Salvation is for sinners and deliverance is for Believers, and sometimes an unsaved person gets both at one time. Our neglect of this much-needed resource is unthinkable. No longer can the Body of Christ ignore the overwhelming need to provide deliverance for the Saints.

My comrades and I on the prayer team at House of Healing—eventually to be called the National Deliverance Center—weekly pray people out of bondage who are having these experiences. We see demons manifest and hear about things people have endured that will turn curly hair straight.

The devil wants to desensitize our children to the things they should be repulsed about or resist. If we are comfortable with elements of darkness, we put ourselves at serious risk for destruction. Society is socializing our children to accept witches, warlocks, and fantasy as innocent forms of entertainment, and it is not. Unfortunately, the devil knows our ignorance to his clever seduction is to his benefit.

In the article "Most Christians Do Not Believe that Satan Or The Holy Spirit Exist" by the Barna Group it revealed, "Four out of ten Christians (40%) strongly agreed that Satan "is not a living being but is a symbol of evil." An additional two out of ten Christians (19%) said they "agree somewhat" with that perspective."[8] The enemy is real even if you think or believe he is not.

There you have it. Believers who do not believe. Is that surprising? It should be. According to the statistics just mentioned the Enemy has outsmarted about 990,000,000 Christians using his number-one skill: deception.

Almost half of the Family of God is duped. He's got them right where he wants them, believing he does not exist. Don't feel bad if the shoe fits, he had me too. I once believed the devil did not exist and people were just using him as an excuse for their mess, but I was wrong. Unbelief is the easiest path to spiritual assassination.

How will we ever be victorious over an enemy we think is an imaginary character? We cannot fight an enemy we do not believe exists. Is it impossible? Until we come into the knowledge of the truth about the rival of God, we are seriously compromised.

The *Modus Operandi* of the Enemy

Let me explain how he operates. Maybe this will help us see what happens when we don't think Satan exists. How about the negative thoughts that keep rolling around in our heads? These common demonic darts are saying … nobody cares about me. I do not matter. I am not important. Do you think those thoughts are ours? Well, they are not.

The enemy of God is concocting those twisted imaginations, perverted distortions—the mental chaos going on in your mind. He wants us to own them. He knows he or his gunnies are the hands throwing the negative and destructive thoughts into our heads.

Unfortunately, too many of us actually do own them, because we do not know the difference. Don't feel bad. There was a time when I did not know the difference either. And, even now, I have to stay on my toes to keep up with his slimy tricks.

The enemy likes to play with our minds, which becomes his territory of torment. Since few in the Body of Christ are taught to discern between our thoughts, God's thoughts, and the thoughts of the enemy, we are being pummeled. Just look around us.

Most of the people—who are emotionally and mentally disturbed—are victims of Satan. We can chalk up child abuse, sexual perversion, addiction, infatuation with pornography and adultery to name a few, to his nature as well. We then become victims of his vicious and calculated assaults.

The enemy is the one who sends the thought God does not love us. He wants us to feel insignificant and unworthy to receive the blessings that have our names on them. He will do anything he can to stop us from pursuing a relationship with Jesus Christ.

He tells so many of us that we are not worthy of anything good, and it is all a lie! He twists things that benefit us so we cannot and will not get them. The enemy wants to violate the mind, crush the heart, and frustrate the dreams of God's people.

Michael W. Smith, not the multi-platinum Christian artist, but the deliverance minister and founder of Hardcore Christianity—simplifies the whole ordeal. This is what he said, "God will never send negative, slanderous, or condemning thoughts about you or anyone else." How simple is that to comprehend?

Once we recognize a spiritual force is dumping trash in our heads, we can slam the door shut and shovel it out as fast as it comes in. We are instructed to take captive every thought and bring it into captivity to the obedience of Christ anyway (2 Corinthians 10:4-5). We have the power to accept or neglect every thought that enters the door of our minds. Now, it takes practice, and in time, it can be as easy as walking.

Helpful information about the Enemy from Scripture:

Who He Is *You were the anointed cherub who covers; I established you; You were on the holy mountain of God; You walked back and forth in the midst of fiery stones (Ezekiel 28:14)*

Where He Lived *You were in Eden, the garden of God; Every precious stone was your covering: The sardius, topaz, and diamond, Beryl, onyx, and jasper, Sapphire, turquoise, and emerald with gold. The workmanship of your timbels and pipes was prepared for you on the day you were created (Ezekiel 28;13)*

What Did He Do *You were perfect in your ways from the day you were created, Till iniquity was found in you. By the abundance of your trading You became filled with violence within, And you sinned (Ezekiel 28:15-16).*

For the devil has come down to you, having great wrath, because he knows that he has a short time (Revelation 12:12)

What Was His Offense *How you are fallen from heaven, O Lucifer son of the morning! How you are cut down to the ground, You who weakened the nations! For you have said in your heart; I will ascend into heaven, I will exalt* *my throne above the stars of God; I will also sit on the mount of the congregation, On the farthest side of the north; I will ascend above the heights of the clouds, I will be like the Most High, Yet you shall be brought down to Sheol, to the lowest depths of the Pit (Isaiah 14:12-15)*

What Was the Result of His Actions *Therefore I cast you as a profane thing Out of the mountain of God; And I destroyed you, O covering cherub, From the midst of the fiery stones. Your heart was lifted up because of your beauty; You corrupted your wisdom for the sake of your splendor; I cast you to the ground, I laid you before kings, That they might gaze at you. You defiled your sanctuaries by the multitude of your iniquities, by the iniquity of your trading; Therefore I brought fire from your midst; It devoured you, And I turned you to ashes upon the earth In the sight of all who saw you (Ezekiel 28: 16-18)*

How Did God Handle His Rebellion Satan and one-third of the angels in Heaven lost their residency that day. *And war broke out in heaven: Michael and his angels fought with the dragon; and the dragon and his angels fought, but they did not prevail, nor was a place found for them in heaven any longer. So the great dragon was cast out, that serpent of old, called the Devil and Satan, who deceives the whole world; he was cast to the earth, and his angels were cast out with him.(Revelation 12:7-9)*

The Structure of His Kingdom *For we do not wrestle against flesh and blood, but against principalities, against powers, against the rulers of the darkness of this age, against spiritual* hosts *of wickedness in the heavenly places (Ephesians 6:12).*

His Demise and Those Like Him
- *And he cast him into the bottomless pit, and shut him up, and set a seal on him, so that he should deceive the nations no more till the thousand years were finished. But after these things he must be released for a little while (Revelations 20:3)*
- *Then the beast was captured, and with him the false prophet who worked signs in his presence, by which he deceived those who received the mark of the beast and those who worshiped his image. These two*

were cast alive into the lake of fire burning with brimstone (Revelations 19:20)

- *And then the lawless one will be revealed, whom the Lord will consume with the breath of His mouth and destroy with the brightness of His coming (2 Thessalonians 2:8)*
- *Then He will also say to those on the left hand, 'Depart from Me, you cursed, into the everlasting fire prepared for the devil and his angels (Matthew 25:41)*
- *Now when the thousand years have expired, Satan will be released from his prison and will go out to deceive the nations which are in the four corners of the earth, Gog and Magog, to gather them together to battle, whose number is as the sand of the sea. They went up on the breadth of the earth and surrounded the camp of the saints and the beloved city. And fire came down from God out of heaven and devoured them. The devil, who deceived them, was cast into the lake of fire and brimstone where the beast and the false prophet are (Revelation 20:7-10)*

How to Protect Ourselves from the Enemy

- *Put on the whole armor of God, that you may be able to stand against the schemes of the devil (Ephesians 6:11)*
- *Therefore submit to God. Resist the devil and he will flee from you (James 4:7)*

Some of His Names

- Before his fall: Lucifer, Angel
- After his fall: Satan, the Devil, Serpent, the Enemy

His Plan is to kill, steal, and destroy (John 10:10)

His Partners are called demons.

DISCIPLE ME NOW: Learn – Grow – Practice - Go

The Truth

- The enemy is not everywhere at one time like God. He uses a complex network of demons who communicate with one another

- *Now the Spirit expressly says that in later times some will depart from the faith, giving heed to deceiving spirits and doctrines of demons (1 Timothy 4:1)*
- *Be sober, be vigilant; because your adversary the devil walks about like a roaring lion, seeking whom he may devour. Resist him, steadfast in the faith, knowing that the same sufferings are experienced by your brotherhood in the world (1 Peter 5:8-9)*
- *You are of your father the devil, and the desires of your father you want to do. He was a murderer from the beginning, and does not stand in the truth, because there is no truth in him. When he speaks a lie, he speaks from his own resources, for he is a liar and the father of it (John 8:44)*
- *He who sins is of the devil, for the devil has sinned from the beginning. For this purpose the Son of God was manifested, that He might destroy the works of the devil (1 John 3:8)*
- *We know that we are of God, and the whole world lies under the sway of the wicked one (1 John 5:19)*
- *Beloved, do not believe every spirit, but test the spirits, whether they are of God; because many false prophets have gone out into the world. By this you know the Spirit of God: Every spirit that confesses that Jesus Christ has come in the flesh is of God, and every spirit that does not confess that Jesus Christ has come in the flesh is not of God. And this is the* spirit *of the Antichrist, which you have heard was coming, and is now already in the world (1 John 4:1-3)*

The Deception
- The enemy can be trusted—FALSE
- The devil cannot affect your children's behavior—FALSE
- If you are a Satan worshiper, the devil likes you—FALSE—His affections are pure manipulations and deceptions to get you to do what he wants
- The enemy has more power than Believers—FALSE—(1 John 4:4)

THE PLAYERS: JESUS

The Savior of the World!

THE TRUTH: Jesus is the Messiah, the Son of God. *For there is one God and one Mediator between God and men, the Man Christ Jesus (1 Timothy 2:5)*

THE DECEPTION: You can have a relationship with God without having a relationship with His Son, Jesus Christ (John 14:6)

Who better to tell us about the Son of the Living God than the Son Himself? He is described using the Son's own words in the famous seven *I Am* Scriptures found in the Book of John. They are amazing.

He says (emphasis mine):

1. ***I AM the bread of Life:*** *He who comes to Me shall never hunger, and he who believes in Me shall never thirst (John 6:35)*

2. ***I AM the Light of the World:*** *He who follows Me shall not walk in darkness, but have the light of life (John 8:12)*

3. ***I AM the Door:*** *If anyone enters by Me, he will be saved, and will go in and out and find pasture (John 10:9)*

4. ***I AM the Good Shepherd:*** *The good shepherd gives His life for the sheep (John 10:11)*

5. ***I AM the resurrection, and the life:*** *He who believes in Me, though he may die shall live. And whoever lives and believes in Me shall never die (John 11:25)*

6. ***I AM the way, the truth, and the life:*** *No one comes to the Father except through Me (John 14:6)*

7. ***I AM the true vine, and My Father is the vinedresser:*** *Every branch in Me that does not bear fruit He takes away; and every branch that bears fruit He prunes, that it may bear more fruit (John 15:1-2)*

The Scripture says, I am the Alpha and the Omega, *the* Beginning and *the* End, the First and the (Revelation 22:13).

Who Did God Say Jesus Was *Then a voice came from heaven, "You are My beloved Son, in whom I am well pleased (Mark 1:11).*

What Did Others Say About who He Was This is who John the Baptist said He was, *The Lamb of God, who takes away the sin of the world (John 1:29)!*

Listen to the conversation between Jesus and His beloved disciple, Peter, about His identity, *Who do men say that I am?" So they answered, "John the Baptist; but some say, Elijah; and others, one of the prophets." He said to them, "But who do you say that I am?" Peter answered and said to Him, "You are the Christ (Mark 8:27-29)*

The Prophet Isaiah said, *For unto us a Child is born, unto us a Son is given; And the government will be upon His shoulder. And His name will be called Wonderful, Counselor, Mighty God, Everlasting Father, Prince of Peace (Isaiah 9:6)*

What Did/Does Jesus Do He is our advocate in Heaven: *It is Christ who died, and furthermore is also risen, who is even at the right hand of God, who also makes intercession for us (Romans 8:34)*

He prays for all Believers to be unified (John 17:23).

How Was Jesus Conceived *After His mother Mary was betrothed to Joseph, before they came together, she was found with child of the Holy Spirit (Matthew 1:18)*

God's Plan for Jesus *For God did not send His Son into the world to condemn the world, but that the world through Him might be saved (John 3:17)*

His Mission Jesus came to reconcile us back to His Father and redeem us from the curse. But, He came for other reasons as well: *For the Son of Man has come to seek and to save that which was lost (Luke 19:10)*

*I have come as a light into the world, that whoever believes in Me should not
abide in darkness (John 12:46)*

*Who was delivered up because of our offenses,
and was raised because of our justification (Romans 4:25)*

*For even the Son of Man did not come to be served, but to serve,
and to give His life a ransom for many (Mark 10:45)*

His Home This is what Jesus said about where He lived: *Jesus answered,
"My kingdom is not of this world. If my kingdom were of this world, My servants would fight, so that I should be delivered to the Jews; but now My kingdom is not here (John 18:36)*

Why did He die for us? He does not want anyone to be lost or separated from
His love. *Not willing that any should perish but that all should come to repentance
(2 Peter 3:9)*

*Even so it is not the will of your Father who is in heaven that one of these
little ones should perish (Matthew 18:14)*

Jesus' Warning *He who is not with Me is against Me, and he who does
not gather with Me scatters abroad (Matthew 12:30)*

How Does Jesus Sustain Himself*My food is to do the will of Him who
sent Me, and to finish His work (John 4:34)*

Do we know Him? We can study Jesus' every waking moment of every
day and still not know Him. We have to know Him for ourselves, not know *of*
Him. If we want to fortify ourselves against the attacks of the enemy, and be
assured of victory, having a relationship with Jesus Christ has to be our number-one priority.

As we begin to build our relationship with Him, we will learn Jesus did
some amazing things. The Scripture says if they were all written, the world
does not have the room to contain it (John 21:25). Personally, my head gets
dizzy just thinking about every time the Word says He healed them all.

I am not a theologian or a student of religious studies. My approach to the most talked about person ever to live is only to keep it simple. Sometimes, religious dogma and denominational superiority makes it confusing about who Jesus is, what He did, why He did it, and what that means to us.

After being converted for real, one of the things I learned quickly is when we are caught in the religious ritual of Church Going and not doing much else, it is very easy to get bored. This is true when we are in an institution that is church focused and not Kingdom focused.

The difference between being church focused and Kingdom focused is *relationship*. In the Kingdom, God has a relationship with His Son, Jesus, and He wants us to have one with Him too. The opposite is often true when people are church focused. They thrive on being activities-driven and not relationship-driven.

History Fuels the Future
On the walls in the first church I attended in Oceanside, California, were pictures of Christian pioneers. At the time, they did not mean much. Now, I understand why our Pastor put them there. When we know our spiritual lineage, it gives us perspective.

Years later, I read, *God's Generals: Why They Succeeded and Why Some Failed* by Roberts Liardon. These books profiled the contributions of the pioneers of Christendom and the challenges they faced. Their stories stirred in me a hunger to know Jesus and live the embodiment of Him the way they did. I wanted the Jesus they knew, and to be used by Him in an unusual way as they were, and nothing seemed to quench that desire.

The people who know their God shall be strong, and carry out great exploits
(Daniel 11:32b)

I was somewhat familiar with the ministry of Kathryn Kuhlman, one of three women mentioned in *God's Generals*. Someone dear to me, named Sara O'Meara, co-founder of Childhelp USA with Yvonne Fedderson, was miraculously healed of terminal cancer at one of her meetings.

Sara and Yvonne have spent a lifetime dedicated to the treatment and prevention of child abuse, which positioned them to be nominated for the Nobel Peace Prize for five consecutive years. Still to this day, I have not seen the likes of Kathryn Kuhlman, who came to Christ at fourteen. She knew Jesus in a way that filled stadiums and changed thousands of lives. I cannot imagine if Sara had not encountered Kathryn.

Jesus Christ is the same yesterday, today, and forever (Hebrews 13:8)

Then I got connected to the lineage of John G. Lake, another General in the book, who was born-again at sixteen. He was known for his healing ministry and missions work in Africa. Lake pioneered the Healing Rooms, which I would come to learn about not long after reading about him. His story energized me the most because of my heart's cry to bless Africa for God's glory.

My first visit to check out the Healing Rooms in Oceanside, California turned into me praying for the two people who prayed for me. As I began to pray, the power of God filled the room and we had to open the door so we could stand. His glory spilled out into the hallway, and before we knew it, His goodness was touching everyone who walked by. Nothing like that had ever happened before.

Our mini-revival became my ticket to being asked to join the Healing Rooms Prayer Team. The Healing Rooms were a beautiful platform to grow in my discernment to hear Jesus' heart for His people. At the time, I was unaware of what Jesus was doing, but at each act of obedience, He was drawing me closer. It was another layer of impartation that was preparing the foundation for something greater.

It seemed I was on the right track, but after reading *God's Generals* it was difficult to reconcile why I had never seen the faith of Smith Wigglesworth, the courage of Jack Coe, or the candor of Maria Woodworth-Etter in the church. I could not help but wonder what are we missing. Where is the revival fire that exploded on Azusa Street under an African American one-eyed Methodist Pastor named William Seymour?

My appetite for experiencing the manifestation of the Kingdom, the way those Believers did, became insatiable. I would not be satisfied until my Jesus, who is no respecter of persons (Acts 10:34), gave me a portion that resembled what I read on those pages.

Although amazing, unprecedented, and rare, these General's successes—and even their challenges—drew me to the source of their motivations: their power and their victories, which was Jesus Himself. Their reckless faith, healing power, and demonstrations were nothing short of how they surrendered their lives to His will. He exposed Himself through them in profound ways. The revelation compelled me to do a most unusual spiritual fast (Isaiah 58).

This fast would not be traditional in the sense of not eating, reading the word and praying. For this purpose I would deliberately study the Word of God differently.

If we want to follow in His steps, we have to lay down our life completely. I needed to know Him in a way I did not. Guided by His Spirit, I commissioned myself to study the life of Jesus, through the Gospel of Matthew, Mark, Luke, and John. For months, I studied, meditated, and read and re-read those books.

Looking at the life of Jesus—as one who desired to be like Him, and do what He did and greater—gave me a provocative perspective I had not seen. His unconditional love, His simplicity of truth, His intentional living to fulfill His assignment, and His compassion for people melted my heart. He loved us unconditionally, completely, and without reservation. His fearlessness to love us, heal, and set us free, meant I could seek to do nothing less if I were to have the portion I was seeking.

Walking in His Steps

Fasting on the life of Jesus made things very clear. My life could no longer be casual. I was determined to be like Jesus everywhere I went. People had to know we are His hands, His feet, and His mouthpiece. They would know He loved them through me. I wanted nothing more than to demonstrate His love and display His power to everyone I met.

But, it wasn't as I thought. This would not be an act of will, something I was accustomed to using. The more I pressed into knowing Him, the more He required of me.

Something shifted in me when my fast ended, but I didn't know it until it manifested at a women's prayer breakfast being held at North Coast Calvary Chapel in Carlsbad, California. The only thing I knew for sure was there had to be less of me and more of Him.

Unbeknownst to me, my new friend Rosa—the woman who spearheaded this move of God—suggested to the church leadership I be the keynote speaker. However, that was quickly squashed because I was not a member of their church. Didn't matter, God had a plan; Rosa was on point, and we both would see His plan unfold.

Upon my arrival at the *Stepping Out in Prayer* Breakfast, a woman I had prayed for during my first visit at the Healing Rooms, came running over to share her praise report. Jesus miraculously healed her tooth pain after I prayed for her. She was so excited. Then she insisted we go into the prayer room, reserved for after the breakfast, and pray for a few women before the event started.

Immediately, the power of God fell and women kept coming in one after another asking us to pray for them. Our commotion started to spill over into the next room. It was apparent something was happening. There was a stirring in the Spirit that had everyone who walked in the room captivated.

We returned to the room next door where the breakfast was being held. As I walked back to my seat, I overheard Rosa saying one of the speakers was not going to make it, and they didn't know what to do. I chimed in and said, "Do you want me to speak?"

They knew if I agreed that meant I would have no time to prepare, but I knew Jesus had something to say; I could feel it in the depths of my being. The speakers were each assigned to one of the Seven Cultural Mountains of Society, created by Bill Bright, founder of Campus Crusade and Loren Cunningham, founder of Youth With a Mission. The mountains included business, government, media, arts and entertainment, education, and family. The last mountain was the religion mountain, which is the one I got.

There is no way that could have been a coincidence. Hence this book, almost seven years later. The stage was set and the room was filled to capacity. Women from all walks of life, races, and religious institutions gathered to pray.

Many of the women attending were not familiar or comfortable with the moving of the Spirit. In hindsight, they were in for an awakening that would change them, and so was I. Needless to say, it was going to be interesting. No matter what, I intended to give them whatever Jesus gave me, undiluted and at full strength.

Every speaker was informative and dynamic and now it was my turn. I was the last person to speak, *ugh* I mean *preach*. All I know is the Holy Spirit came through me like a mighty rushing wind. If my flesh wanted to get in the way, it did not have a chance. My mouth opened and the words flew out like fire.

Women started jumping out of their chairs yelling amen, all right, some were shaking, and others were crying. We could feel the spiritual current in the room as the women embraced the fire. It was explosive and glorious all at the same time.

My prayer had been answered, and my fast was consummated with the power of Pentecost rising up right in the middle of Calvary Chapel. The same virtue that had been pulled from Jesus' body when the woman with the issue of blood touched the hem of His garment was now cascading over every woman at the breakfast. In a small and meaningful way, Jesus did in me what He did in the trailblazers in *God's Generals*, and the wick of revival was re-ignited.

The Perpetual Sacrifice

When we stand before Jesus, He will not be talking about most of what we think is important. On this path of building a relationship with Him, I've been down a few rabbit trails, but I'm all the wiser because of it. None of us get it right all the time. We need grace for when we do mess up, and we will mess up.

We have to know who Jesus is and why we serve Him, because the enemy and his homies are on a mission to shift our loyalties. Steven Covey is famous for saying, "Begin with the end in mind." When we know why Jesus did what He did, it will strengthen our relationship with Him. Then it is not so easy to be swayed from His promise.

Jesus left the comforts of His Kingdom and the luxuries of His life and came to earth. The Bible says the earth is His footstool, so He did not have to go far (Acts 7:49).

For this purpose the Son of God was manifested, that He might
destroy the works of the devil (1 John 3:8)

DISCIPLE ME NOW: Learn – Grow - Practice - Go
The Truth
- Jesus, God, and the Holy Spirit are one (John 10:30)
- Jesus is the Messiah the Jews are waiting for (John 10:33-39)
- *Jesus Christ is the same yesterday, today and forever (Hebrews 13:8)*
- There is salvation in His name (Romans 10:13)

- *Therefore God also has highly exalted Him and given Him the name which is above every name, that at the name of Jesus every knee should bow, of those in heaven, and of those on earth, and of those under the earth, and that every tongue should confess that Jesus Christ is Lord, to the glory of God the Father (Philippians 2:9-11)*
- There is power in His name (Jeremiah 10:6)
- His name cleanses: *And such were some of you. But you were washed, but you were sanctified, but you were justified in the name of the Lord Jesus and by the Spirit of our God (1 Corinthians 6:11)*
- You can heal and perform miracles in His name: *By stretching out your hand to heal, and that signs and wonders may be done through the name of Your holy servant Jesus (Acts 4:30)*
- Casting out demons is done in His name: *Then the seventy returned with joy, saying, "Lord, even the demons are subject unto us in your name (Luke 10:17)*
- *Let this mind be in you which was also in Christ Jesus, who, being in the form of God, did not consider it robbery to be equal with God, but made Himself of no reputation, taking the form of a bondservant, and coming in the likeness of men (Philippians 2:5-7)*
- If you love me, keep My commandments (John 14:15)
- *Therefore if the Son makes you free, you shall be free indeed (John 8:36)*

The Deceptions
- There are many routes to God and Jesus is not the only way—FALSE
- We do not need to have a relationship with Jesus—FALSE
- Jesus is dead—FALSE
- Jesus did not rise from the grave—FALSE
- Jesus has left those who have turned their back on Him—FALSE
- There are no consequences for not believing Jesus is the Messiah—FALSE—*Therefore I said to you that you will die in your sins; for if you do not believe that I am He, you will die in your sins (John 8:24)*
- The Mother of Jesus is a Saint—FALSE
- You cannot talk to Jesus directly. You must use a Priest to speak for you. FALSE (Hebrew 10:19-22)
- Jesus the Messiah has not come—FALSE

- Jesus is only a prophet—FALSE
- Jesus is a fictional character—FALSE

THE PLAYERS: **THE KINGDOM OF GOD**

God's People, in God's Place, Under God's Rule[9]

THE TRUTH: *For the kingdom of God (KOG) is not in word but in power (1 Corinthians 4:20)*
THE DECEPTION: The Kingdom of Darkness (KOD)

As Christians, do we know what it means to be part of the Kingdom, and why it is important? My intention here is to introduce us to the basics about the Kingdom of God—and its rival, the Kingdom of Darkness. This general overview can jumpstart our spiritual engines, or be a refresher, and equip us to at least begin to understand the difference between the two.

Can we distinguish if we are operating in one Kingdom or the other? The first time I really understood the term "Kingdom of God" was after having a life-altering conversion experience, and I was over forty. My childhood beliefs in Christendom became a reality at one of the most pivotal moments of my life.

A few weeks after my conversion, I had the Bible in my hand wondering how I would consume, digest, and regurgitate all that was in it. The thought was overwhelming. At that moment, Matthew 6:33, which says, *"But seek first the kingdom of God and His righteousness, and all these things shall be added to you,"* was pressed upon my heart.

Let me transparent, at that time in my life my focus was on pursuing the American dream. Yes, I was relieved when God gave me His strategy for success. God knows what language we speak. In all reality, I had no idea what that meant.

If I were being completely honest, I think I skated right over "Kingdom of God" and zeroed in on "His righteousness," with more attention focused on what He was going to be adding. Have you heard the Kingdom of God preached about in any way—outside of reading a Scripture?

There is no doubt in my mind Matthew 6:33 is one of the most strategic verses for disciples. This Scripture is like a spiritual narcotic and it falls into the category of hardcore manna. We need teeth to chew it and a supernatural chaser to swallow it down.

Once this Word was planted in my heart, it began to yield a bountiful return. This verse alone has driven my relationship with God to heights I never imagined. It is always in the forefront of my mind. I also try to share it with as many people as possible. It would be selfish to keep all this goodness a secret.

A Real Kingdom Clashes

Here is how God helped me to understand *kingdom*. Until 2009, as an American, it was difficult for me to grasp the whole *kingdom* concept. But, in September of that year I led a missions trip to Uganda, and we landed in the middle of a civil disagreement between the President of Uganda, Yoweri Museveni and the supporters of Bugandan King, Ronald Mutebi.

Our destination was a rural village, about four hours from the capital city of Kampala. The fighting was along the routes we traveled, and by the grace of God, we made it through right before it spilled over into the streets.

The King was to attend a rally in another district, and the attempt to stop him cost several people their lives. In an article in the Economist on September 16, 2009 it described, the riots as "a row with the Buganda region over aspirations of self-government." The article claims, "the Kayunga district is home to the Banyala ethnic group, which is trying to secede from the kingdom of Buganda."[10]

At the time of this incident, Uganda had four ancient kingdoms, of which Buganda's tribal members are the largest ethnic group. Each kingdom has its own king, and the king has his own government, rules, and activities. The buck stops with the king; so when another government attempts to tell a king what he can, or cannot do, we can expect conflict.

It was not until I had experienced a clash of rulers firsthand that I really understood the Kingdom of God. It was a perfect spiritual picture of Kingdom rule, dominion, authority, and territory. Two kingdoms cannot mutually co-exist in the same space. One will inevitably dominate the other, and that is usually determined by loyalty or force, and sometimes money. There is no such thing as shared rulership.

*No one can serve two masters; for either he will hate the one and love the
other, or else he will be loyal to the one and despise the other (Matthew 6:24)*

When I left Uganda, doing missions work and the new revelation on the
Kingdom of God altered my perspective on everything. In light of the tragic
events, my decision to invite people on a mission trip would no longer be
casual.

About the Kingdom of God

*The Lord has established His throne in heaven, and His kingdom rules over
all (Psalm 103:19)*

Everyone who professes to be part of the Kingdom of God is subject to
the King's rulership. Our King is God the Father, who is the King of kings.
Learning about the Kingdom of God should be a priority.

The Kingdom of God and the Kingdom of Heaven are two terms used in
Scripture that are interchangeable, but I found a definition that gives a nice
distinction between the two.

In the book, *The Kingdom of Power: How to Demonstrate It Here & Now*
by Guillermo Maldonado, he says The Kingdom of God is the atmosphere pro-
duced by our relationship of obedience and submission to Him. The Kingdom
of Heaven is, a spiritual location called "heaven" from which God rules and
influences the earth and the entire universe. This is God's dwelling place or
atmosphere where His throne, court of angels, elders, and so forth are found
(Revelation 4:9-10).[11]

Millions of church people know nothing about kingdom living, and there
is a difference. Going to church does not make you kingdom minded, and neither does it equip you with what you need to possess the kingdom.

Kingdom people must occupy until Jesus comes—take it by force, wrestle
with wickedness in high places, and know we have dominion, power, and authority to rule. Not on the backside of the rapture either, right now. Jimm Botts
said it perfectly, "*The Kingdom is not a means to a bigger church; the church
is a means to demonstrating the Kingdom!*"

Is the Kingdom of God being demonstrated through us, the church? If it is
not, the change can come as quickly as we decide to be the people that it can be

demonstrated through. This is not a moment to "pass the buck." If we've been waiting for our Esther moment—here it is. You are reading this book because your steps are ordered and you are being provoked for a time such as this.

Now, if you are anything like me, you have to be asking, "So, how exactly do we demonstrate the Kingdom of God?" Brilliant question because we should all know how to bring Heaven to Earth.

The Kingdom of God is not observed. It is demonstrated, which means shown, made known, experienced, or encountered through experience. Every time Jesus said the Kingdom has come, it was in the face of something extraordinary and supernatural happening. Although His demonstrations were undeniable the religious leaders tried to discredit Him with vicious lies and mass manipulations. We will experience the same thing.

Whenever sin is revealed, renounced, or repented of, people are healed, demons are cast out, and the dead are raised—the Kingdom has come. Now we know why I tried to raise Neicey from the dead. I wanted to bring Heaven to earth and demonstrate the Kingdom. Love, forgiveness, compassion, grace, and mercy are manifestations of the Kingdom too.

Remember, there is no lack in God's Kingdom. No sickness. No pain. No poverty. No separation. In His Kingdom, there is perfect peace, harmony, unconditional love, complete truth, unlimited provision, and divine order. Our jobs as Believers are to be the conduits to bring these things into the atmosphere that we are in. Got it?

Our presence should cause a stir just like when Jesus walked the earth—as the light is supposed to provoke the darkness. When true born-again, baptized, and spirit-filled Believers come around demons should manifest, and we keep wondering why people act so bad every time we show up. Now we know. The light should expose the darkness.

The sick should be getting well; the dead should be rising; sin should be exposed, and poverty should cease. Jesus lacked nothing—so why do we as Kingdom connoisseurs? He did not have an abundance of stored wealth. He was not an athlete, celebrity, or entertainer with the resources to do whatever He wanted. Although he was God incarnate, he was flesh with the same magnitude of power we carry as vessels to do what He did.

According to Got Questions Ministries, "More narrowly, the Kingdom of God is a spiritual rule over the hearts and lives of those who willingly submit to God's authority. Those who defy God's authority and refuse to submit to

Him are not part of the Kingdom of God; in contrast, those who acknowledge the Lordship of Christ and gladly surrender to God's rule in their hearts are part of the Kingdom of God."[12]

The Kingdom of God Is...
- At hand, repent and believe (Mark 1:15)
- *Not eating and drinking, but righteousness and peace and joy in the Holy Spirit (Romans 14:17)*
- An everlasting Kingdom that endures through all generations (Psalm 145:13)
- *Is not of this world (John 18:36)*
- Righteousness, justice, mercy and truth (Psalm 89:14)

Jesus used seven parables in Matthew thirteen to teach about the Kingdom of God. He knew those who were not of His Kingdom would not understand. A parable is a simple story that illustrates a lesson of moral or spiritual significance (Luke 8:10). Read them, study their meanings, and meditate on how we can manifest them in our lives.

In verse fifty-one of Matthew thirteen, Jesus asked them:"Have you understood all these things?" Which of these parables do you understand?

Check all that apply to you: 1. ❑   2. ❑   3. ❑   4. ❑   5. ❑   6. ❑   7. ❑

1. **The Parable of the Sower**—The gospel of the Kingdom will encounter four conditions of a person's heart when it is preached. Which ground describes the condition of your heart?
    ❑ Wayside   ❑ Stony   ❑ Thorny   ❑ Good

2. **The Parable of the Wheat and Tares**—It is difficult to distinguish God's children from the children of the world. Which one are you? Are you wheat acting like a tare? ❑ Yes   ❑ No

3. **The Parable of the Mustard Seed**—The Kingdom of God might look small right now, but in the end, it will be great. Are you aware our time on earth is temporary and very short compared to eternity? ❑ Yes   ❑ No

4. **The Parable of the Leaven**—The Kingdom is in operation as we speak and in due season we will see the fullness of it. Do you know that everything about the Kingdom of God has not been revealed yet? ❑ Yes ❑ No

5. **The Parable of the Hidden Treasurer**—One must be willing to part with all he has to possess the Kingdom. Identify one or two things you have or had a difficult time letting go of to possess the Kingdom of God.
   1. _____ 2. _____

6. **The Parable of the Pearl of Great Price**—The Kingdom is worth everything you have. Jesus gave everything He had. Are you willing to give up everything to have what God has for you? ❑ Yes ❑ No

7. **The Parable of the Dragnet**—The gospel must be shared with all, although some will not receive it. Can you handle people not accepting the Good News—knowing one man sows, another waters, but God is the one who provides the increase? ❑ Yes ❑ No

There are a total of forty parables in the Bible, of which nineteen are directly related to the Kingdom. We have engaged in seven. Can you find the other twelve parables? Search for them with a friend who also wants to grow in their faith.

The Lord's Prayer in Matthew 6:10 says, "*My kingdom come and my will be done on earth as it is in heaven.*" The only way that is going to happen is through us. We are the vessles for the Kingdom of God to come to forth.

Where Is the Kingdom of God
- *Behold, the tabernacle of God is with men, and He will dwell with them, and they shall be His people. God himself will be with them and be their God(Revelation 21:3)*

How to Enter the Kingdom of God
- *Receive it like a child (Mark 10:15)*
- *Through many tribulations (Acts 14:22)*

Who Will Enter the Kingdom of God
- *Those who are born-again (John 3:3)*
- *Those born of water and the Spirit (John 3:5)*
- *Those who do the will of the Father (Matthew 7:21)*
- *Those who are the poor in spirit (Matthew 5:3)*
- *The children (Matthew 19:14)*

Who *Will Not* Enter the Kingdom of God
- Unbelievers (Matthew 21:31)
- Flesh and blood (1 Corinthians 15:50)
- *Not everyone who says to Me, 'Lord, Lord(Matthew 7:21)*
- The unrighteous. *Neither fornicators, nor idolaters, nor adulterers, nor effeminate, nor homosexuals, nor thieves, nor the covetous, nor drunkards, nor revilers, nor swindlers (1 Corinthians 6:9-10)*
- *Deeds of the flesh, which are: immorality, impurity, sensuality, idolatry, sorcery, enmities, strife, jealousy, outbursts of anger, disputes, dissensions, factions, envying, drunkenness, carousing, and things like these (Galatians 5:19-21)*
- *No immoral or impure person or covetous man, who is an idolater (Ephesians 5:5)*
- *Unless your righteousness surpasses that of the scribes and Pharisees, you will not enter the kingdom of heaven (Matthew 5:20)*

The Kingdom of Darkness
The Kingdom of Darkness mimics the Kingdom of God to create confusion. This Kingdom is not eternal like the Kingdom of God. It has an end and it will be brutal.

This Kingdom operates using deceptive practices, satanic strategies, occultism, false religions, and rhetoric. The king of this Kingdom is power-hungry, a con, a liar, and a thief. To fuel his Kingdom, he will use whatever he can—including, but not limited to—fear, control, and deception. When we indulge his practices, it may appear we are taking a shortcut to fulfill our dreams, realize our potential, or make progress. In actuality, we are only taking a detour.

Not everything that looks like God is behind it, is God. Everyone must come through the door.

Most assuredly, I say to you, he who does not enter the sheepfold by the door, but climbs up some other way, the same is a thief and a robber (John 10:1)

Using the of Kingdom of Darkness as a platform to advance in the Kingdom of God is unethical. For example, reading our daily horoscope to predict our future —we call witchcraft. It is designed to lead us down a rabbit trail.

When we have a strong relationship with God and His people, we do not channel what is classified as familiar spirits. Familiar spirits are just that: spirits that are familiar (Leviticus 20:6). They have information about you. The Bible says do not do this, because it can be done. Choose you this day which Kingdom you are going to be a part of—and it cannot be both.

"Give no regard to mediums and familiar spirits; do not seek after them, to be defiled by them"(Leviticus 19:31)

Fraternizing with this arena called familiar spirits is not innocent (Deuteronomy 18:9-12). When we subject ourselves to horoscopes, palm readers, and channeling, the intent in the Kingdom of Darkness is to alter our spiritual destinies and destroy our health. We are now contaminated, and there is a price to pay for being infected with these spirits.

The agents of darkness are operating in the world, and they are also positioned in the church.

For such are false apostles, deceitful workers, transforming themselves into apostles of Christ. And no wonder! For Satan himself transforms himself into an angel of light. Therefore it is no great thing if his ministers also transform themselves into ministers of righteousness, whose end will be according to their works (2 Corinthians 11:13–15)

It is important for us to be able to identify the wolves in sheep's clothing.

Beware of false prophets, who come to you in sheep's clothing, but inwardly they are ravenous wolves (Matthew 7:15)

The Kingdom of God imposes on the Kingdom of Darkness, although God has given Satan rule over the earth. It takes a violent assault to push back the Kingdom of Darkness. The Scripture says it like this:

And from the days of John the Baptist until now the kingdom of heaven suffers violence, and the violent take it by force (Matthew 11:12)

His Kingdom is propagated by pride, unbelief, and lies. The pride is when he is trying to be something he is not, which is God. The unbelief is his inability to walk in truth. He knows the truth, because he was once there with God.

Every lie we believe is demonic yardage. We have to take back what is stolen through our agreements with his deceptions. Allow God to replace what was taken and rebuild what was destroyed.

He will twist the Word of God just enough to make us think what is being said is true. He creates confusion and confusion is not of God. Remember, a little leaven is enough to change the shape of the whole thing (Galatians 5:9). We have to distinguish false doctrine by the power of the Holy Spirit.

Everything about the Kingdom of Darkness is designed to deceive us. His deception begins first with him. He can disguise himself as an angel of light. Why? Because, if we could see his motives, we would be repelled.

He pumps us up because he knows it is an offense to God. He wants us to be like him: prideful, arrogant, and even haughty. All we have to remember is the nature of darkness is the opposite of the nature of God.

Then he takes his madness to extremes when he invades the subconscious mind. Yes, he can give us demonic dreams and visions. The whole dream invasion is an assault against the future God has for His heirs—and a calculated effort to molest the prophecies in the Book of Joel. This is an attempt to sow seeds of diversion to the coming revival.

And it shall come to pass afterward That I will pour out My Spirit on all flesh; Your sons and your daughters shall prophesy, Your old men shall dream dreams, Your young men shall see visions (Joel 2:28)

His kingdom will end. *The devil, who deceived them, cast into the lake of fire and brimstone where the beast and the false prophet are. And they will be tormented day and night forever and ever (Revelation 20:10)*

Rid Your Dwelling of Darkness

Several years ago, I made contact with a former roommate. It had been many years since we talked. Our reunion turned into a divine appointment. We both went to church and knew the Lord when we lived together, but we were average Christians doing our own thing and churching it on Sundays. The last thing I expected to be doing when I saw her was exorcizing her house.

In our brief conversation, she revealed she was having strange activities in her home, especially at night. She also said it was difficult for her to sleep, which can sometimes be the result of your environment being saturated with sin, negative activities, or material possessions associated with darkness.

She insisted I come over and help her get her house in spiritual order. To my surprise, shortly after talking to her, I got a call from one of my spiritual mentors. We often ended up in town at the same time. She was driving less than a mile away from where I was. Of course, I coaxed her into coming over and giving me a hand.

I had no idea how steeped my former roomy was in demonic religious artifacts. When I arrived, the first thing that caught my attention was a gold sculpted Buddha about two feet tall at the front door. Instantly, I remembered my former roommate was an interior designer who only enjoyed the finest of furnishings and accents. The question circled my mind, "Is she ready for what needs to be done?" Five hours later, I got my answer. She was.

This is what we did. I always carry anointing oil in my purse, and I always seem to need it. We took off our shoes and anointed the bottoms of our feet. We covered the house in prayer and tried to bind everything that would attempt to manifest while we were getting rid of stuff.

I invited the lady of the house to lead the way. She was to identify the items she thought needed to go. If she had questions, we would answer. At the end of the day, if a person still has an attachment to something in their heart, they might as well keep it (Matthew 5:28). She decided if it stayed or went, not us.

We went from the living room, to the office, down the hallway, to the bedroom, into the bathroom, through the kitchen, and ended in the dining room. No matter where she was in her spiritual journey—because we were in agreement and all on one accord—the Holy Spirit led us to the cracks and crevices of her house. There we retrieved demonic relics disturbing the atmosphere.

She opened drawers and cabinets where we found miniature Buddha's. I believe she had them for good luck. Christians do not subscribe to good luck.

We do favor and blessings. Anything that has to be hidden should be questioned anyway.

She threw away nice sheets she shared with former lovers. She had paintings on the walls that were expensive, but she said take them, and we did. There are very few things with a snake on it that a Christian should want to possess. Decorations or sculptures with more than one head are a sure candidate for destruction and she had some.

We took a few breaks to take things to the garbage dumpster. I know we made at least seven trips to discard thousands of dollars of nice, but demonic, stuff. We told my roomy to stay in the house when we walked to the trash.

We did not want her to see us throwing her stuff away and cause her to change her mind. The enemy will do that to you. We ripped, beat, and smashed it to a pulp as we threw it in. We made sure she would not be able to come back in the morning and get it, and neither would anyone else.

House Cleaning Gone Bad

Shortly after my real conversion I did my own spiritual house cleaning and put everything that had to go out by the dumpster. Less than fifteen minutes later all of it was taken. Sadly, I gave my spiritual baggage to someone else. If I had known better, I would have done different. It is not wise to give demonic stuff away—causing someone else to suffer or to profit from it. Would Jesus put the idols the Israelites worshipped on eBay?

I checked on my old roomy the next day, and she said there was a drastic difference in her house. She slept better than she had in years. On a personal note, I was a bit freaked out about how much we trashed. I was not sure how she was going to handle what we did. Fortunately, she was fine and all the better because of it.

Not only do our lives, characters, and behaviors need to line up with the Kingdom of God, but our dwellings do too. We will find ourselves in utter shock to know the number of things currently in our homes that could be sabotaging our maturity and hindering our spiritual progress.

Evil prevails when Christians do not use the power we have, or the authority we've been given as part of the Kingdom of God.

"The only thing necessary for the triumph of evil is for good men to do nothing."
Edmund Burke

DISCIPLE ME NOW: Learn – Grow – Practice - Go

The Truth

- Have no fellowship with darkness (Ephesians 5:11)
- *Do not be unequally yoked together with unbelievers. For what fellowship has righteousness with lawlessness? And what communion has light with darkness? And what accord has Christ with Belial? Or what part has a believer with an unbeliever (2 Corinthians 6:14)?"*

A Simple Do-It-Yourself Strategy for Spiritual Housecleaning

We can do spiritual housecleaning as a family activity or alone, and we do not need a Priest. God has given us the authority to tread on scorpions. This is also a perfect opportunity to engage your spouse, children, relatives and/or friends.

Give everyone an opportunity to discern what needs to go, and why or why not. Incorporate the Scriptures into the process. Discuss letting go of material things to make room to possess the Kingdom of God and all it has to offer. We must be sure to do it in love and not in condemnation—no matter what we find in our homes or someone else's.

1. Get yourself some anointing oil or you can buy olive oil at your local grocery and use it the same way. Bless your oil by praying over it and ask God to anoint it with His supernatural power; pray it will be effective in anything you use it for; you do not need to do anything more. It is good to always keep a bottle of anointing oil in your home

2. You have to repent for any involvement in the Kingdom of Darkness; ask God to reveal any connections, associations, or items you may have before you start

3. Tell God you are genuinely sorry for disobeying His Word, even if you did not know until now; ignorance is not an excuse for participation

4. Renounce any demonic agreements you made knowingly or unknowingly; for example, if you made an agreement in your heart to hate someone who hurt you—you created a tie to the Kingdom of Darkness and it must be severed

5. Tell the enemy you no longer agree to engage in the things of his King-
    dom, and you sever all ties, agreements, and sealed arrangements
6. Stand proxy and repent for the sins of your parents and those before them
    that may have opened the door to your propensity to lean toward darkness
7. Identify your starting point in your home
8. You cannot dictate what should stay or go for your spouse, but you do have
    the spiritual authority to say so for your underage children. Note: It is not
    appropriate to spiritually clean or insist that a home that is not yours be
    cleaned. If you do not like what is going on in someone else's home then
    the righteous thing to do is leave or move.
9. Pray for increased discernment, spiritual vision, and wisdom as you make
    your way through every room
10. Get rid of everything associated with darkness including books, CDs, jew-
    elry, memberships, clothing, or special paraphernalia. Destroy it; do not
    toss it; the enemy will send someone to recover what you have thrown
    away so it can continue to be used
11. Anoint your entire dwelling once everything has been confiscated and de-
    stroyed; command every spirit not of God to leave your home and every
    spiritual door opened through your association and activities to be closed
    permanently
12. In each room declare it is saturated in the blood of Jesus. Bind every spirit
    not of God. Command every high thing of darkness to come down and be
    subject to the plan of God for every occupant. Speak that your dwelling is
    Holy ground protected by God.
13. Go around to every entryway and seal it with the blood of Jesus by lightly
    drawing a cross, in oil, over every window, door and opening to the out-
    side; you can take it a step further and go outside to the parameter of your
    home and pour a few drops of anointing oil in the four corners; I prayed
    for my house to be protected from invasion or harm
14. Last, open the front or back door to the outside and command every spirit
    not of God to go. Then call in the Holy Spirit to occupy every ounce of
    space. Finish by declaring a hedge of Holy Ghost fire protecting your
    house

Now, for some of us, this is going to be a breeze. We are excited to finally
know the truth and to be set free from the wiles of the devil. For others this will
be a serious process of dying to our flesh and possessions.

We might think the value of what we are tossing is significant. We may want to sell it and retrieve a financial benefit and not experience a complete loss. Or, we could have tremendous sentimental value to our stuff, I did. Whichever the case, let's be reminded why we are doing what we are doing.

When we know the potential threat we are harboring, it is easier to release what God has expressed is an abomination to Him. We have to hate what God hates and love what He loves. If you have trouble with this activity, ask the Holy Spirit to give you the strength to fulfill this necessary assignment. He is faithful to answer. Be like Jesus and do what pleases the Father and not the flesh.

The Deception
- The Kingdom of Darkness is not real—FALSE
- There is no harm in practicing witchcraft by using items such as Ouija Boards, crystals, and tarot cards—FALSE
- Darkness is not contagious—FALSE—*Do not be deceived: "evil company corrupts good habits" (1 Corinthians 15:33)*
- Deeds of darkness will not be exposed—FALSE—*And this is the condemnation, that the light has come into the world, and men loved darkness rather than light, because their deeds were evil. For everyone practicing evil hates the light and does not come to the light, lest his deeds should be exposed. But he who does the truth comes to the light, that his deeds may be clearly seen, that they have been done in God (John 3:19-21)*
- Perversion can be compartmentalized or isolated—FALSE—*But, if your eye is bad, your whole body will be full of darkness. If therefore the light that is in you is darkness, how great is that darkness (Matthew 6:23)*

THE PLAYERS: **THE CHRISTIAN** (Believer)

Followers of Christ!

THE TRUTH: *He who believes and is baptized will be saved; but he who does not believe will be condemned (Mark 16:16)*
THE DECEPTION: You do not have to change once you are born-again

The Apology

There are a lot of wounded people who go to church, and many others who were hurt by people in the church and now they don't go to church. At some point, we have all been hurt by somebody, some more deeply than others. But, I know getting hurt by church folk seems to pack more of a punch.

Sadly, there are too many people leaving the church because they got offended. Then there are those of us who never left, but we carry open sores and it is adversely affecting our behavior. In either case, whatever happened that hurt you warrants an apology—especially if you never got one.

On behalf of the people who hurt you—especially those in the church— and never humbled themselves to say I'm sorry, let me say it for them:

I am so sorry you got hurt in the place you thought you would be safe, and that you had or are having a bad experience in God's house or at the hands of God's people. You getting hurt was not His plan, but it does happen and you can overcome it and heal. God wants you to follow His guidelines and forgive them, release them, and pray for them according to Matthew 5:44. This is necessary for you to gain full access to your spiritual inheritance. God wants you to be free to live the extraordinary life He has planned for you.

Do you receive what I am saying? If so, then let the offense go and move on by faith. Forgiveness is a supernatural act, and the power of the Holy Spirit is here right now to assist you in what you may have felt was impossible. He is in the business of doing what we cannot.

Say this with me, "Father, by faith, I release those who have wounded my Spirit, attempted to destroy my destiny, or hurt me in any way. Forgive me, God, for not forgiving them sooner, and having bad feelings toward them. Today, I bind all the darkness in me and I command it to let go of my emotions in the name of Jesus. Father, fill those now-empty places with grace, love, peace, mercy, kindness, patience, tolerance, and joy. I declare that I am now healed and I receive all that is good in Jesus' name. Amen.

Not take a deep breath and exhale all the memories, the pain, and the disappointment. Bravo! When we do this it clears the path to our promise. Now, receive by faith everything God has for you. Un-forgiveness and offense can no longer hinder our maturity or block our progress.

Are we Christians? How do we know? Research concludes—upon examination of the two point two billion Christians as a whole—in fact, many of them do not subscribe to the basics of their faith. After Believers make confessions of faith, many of them do not change. They continue in their carnal ways. Is that a deception issue, a discipleship dilemma, or both?

There are four distinct conversion episodes in my Christian walk. I was baptized around eleven or twelve, at Mount Carmel Missionary Baptist Church in Milwaukee, Wisconsin. For some reason, I cannot recall why I got baptized, but I know why we should be baptized. What I remember most about my baptism is being scared to death standing in front of all those people saying I wanted to be baptized.

It might be a good guess I got baptized out of emotion and not conviction, because nothing changed in my life as a result of it. My outward demonstration of an inward decision faded fast. By the time I was fourteen, I was smoking cigarettes, stealing from the grocery store, and headed toward being a teen parent like some of my friends.

The International Bible Society said eighty-three percent of all Christians make their commitment to Jesus between the ages of four and fourteen, which is now referred to as the "four to fourteen window." The salvation statistics for fourteen to eighteen-year-olds who accept Jesus drops to four percent. It is smart thinking to invest your evangelism dollars in targeting children fourteen and younger.

The second exchange happened when I was fifteen or sixteen. My cousin came to visit one summer from Louisiana. She was a born-again Believer who was on fire for the Lord. It was the first and last time someone witnessed to me. Nobody said "Okay, now you're saved, and here are the things you need to know, do, work on, practice … nothing. My cousin went back to Louisiana, and I was left to figure things out for myself.

Giving our lives to Christ is the most important decision we will ever make. It is more significant than getting married and having children. We might think holding the office of President of the USA—the most powerful office in the world—is more important than getting saved, but it isn't.

Accepting Christ as our Lord and Savior is also about securing where we will spend eternity. My last year of high school, all I did was go to church, shout or should I say practice emotionalism, sing, and go to church some more.

My memories tell me it was fun, but when I look back I am baffled at how my time was spent. *Going to church* kept me out of trouble for sure, but I also know what God intended for His children is more than Church Going. When do we get to the part about being made a disciple and the compelling them to come?

Needless to say, that didn't last long. There was nothing to sustain me in the face of every enticing mentionable coming from the world. Because I had never been discipled or spirit-filled—it meant a sheep was about to go astray... again. Christians are not cattle; we are sheep, and sheep wander if they are not properly shepherded, especially if they are young and impressionable.

When I graduated from high school and started working, the cares of this world eventually had their way. Anyone who is not spirit-filled is easy prey for darkness. Slowly, my life slid back into the routine of sin. I disappeared off the Holy-Roller radar, and nobody cared or called.

On September 11, 2001 I dropped to my knees for the third time. My boyfriend woke me up to tell me one of the towers at the World Trade Center was hit by a plane. Along with the rest of the world, I watched in horror as the second plane hit the other tower shortly after the first. I was in shock.

All day, my mind kept replaying how thousands of people got up that morning and were dead by noon. People were instantly orphaned, widowed, blinded, maimed, childless, and devastated. Who didn't have some measure of PTSD after hearing about all the firefighters, police officers, and the port-authority personnel buried in the rubble? We saw people jump out of windows, overtaken by smoke, and sheer pandemonium, with nowhere to hide. It was overwhelming.

My heart sank, over and over again, and each time it did, the fear in me grew. It was the thought of dying suddenly and knowing I was backslidden or maybe I never really got saved. The possibility of missing Heaven, and spending eternity in Hell, had me asking God to save me, yet again. But, fear was not enough to hold me. The prodigal daughter continued in her wicked ways and was at risk of eternal death, every minute, of every day, again for the next two decades.

There is much debate about *once saved, always saved.* It is true, no one can snatch you out of the hand of God, but you can jump.

What shall we say then? Shall we continue in sin that grace may abound?
Certainly not! How shall we who died to sin live any longer in it
(Romans 6:1-2)

I guess the question we have to ask ourselves is were we ever saved in the beginning? The first time I confessed, I do not believe I got saved. I feel I went through the motions. The second time, I really wanted to be saved. And, the third time I was driven by fear, which is not of God, and my confession only lasted a few weeks.

My fourth conversion was wild, unexpected, and downright life-altering. I prayed a short prayer on my way to practicing the religious ritual of Sunday Church Going, that changed the trajectory of my life. God answered within five minutes, and I was devastated by how He did it.

I was on the cusp of launching my own television talk show. The pilot had already aired on CBS. Shortly after my prayer I got a telephone call canceling an interview that was scheduled for the next day. The interview was for a magazine cover story scheduled the month before my show would start airing. The cancellation had a domino affect that shattered my dream of hosting a charitable showcase on television. When the dust settled I was on the path God intended for me before the foundation of the world, and eventually I was very happy about it.

Suddenly every comfort that I was accustomed to was gone, and everything I was familiar with, including my family and all my friends went with it. I was put on the road to my destiny, and it cost me everything.

No man can come unto Him unless he is drawn (John 6:44). Finally, my King had come shifting everything in His path to get to me. However, I did not know exactly what He was doing. It felt as though He was trying to kill me.

When I finally recovered from being apprehended everything was different, and without question, I was saved.

The New Place of Residence

Now you know how I got saved. How did you get saved? I have spoken to people who have defined attending church as a salvation experience. When we make a confession of faith, it is a defining moment. Going to church does not make one saved, but saved folk do go to church.

Here are some things to think about to evaluate if you actually did have a true conversion. Did someone tell you about Jesus Christ? We call that witnessing. Did you have a life-altering experience? Maybe you told God, "If you do this ... I'll do that" meaning giving your life to Him? Ultimatums are usually fear-driven. Do you recall the Lord speaking to your heart, and calling you out of darkness and into the splendid light?

Maybe you were at church, or a conference, on a mission's trip and someone did a call for salvation. Make sure your salvation experience is biblical, not just emotional. The latter usually coincides with no changes in your life or behavior post confession.

When we make a true confession of faith, it is evidenced by not only a changed life, but a renewed mind, and a transformed heart. Suddenly and supernaturally, old things have passed away and everything becomes news (2 Corinthians 5:17). This is not a cliché.

After the forth confession people wondered if I did something to my hair. My cousin looked at me like I was an alien because I kept talking about Jesus. The reality was something happened in my heart. Suddenly, the loose lips that sink ships had a restraint on them. On the inside I knew I was different, changed—new in a way I had never experienced.

My thoughts shifted from what I wanted in life, to what God wanted for me. Instantly, the world was bigger because it was not just about *me* anymore. A hunger to know God kept driving me toward Him. The King of kings, the God of the Israelites, and One who parted the Red Sea, was now not only my Savior, but also my Lord and Master.

The physical location of where I lived changed, and so did my spiritual address. The television show I hoped to syndicate was the carnage of a simple request to God to line me up with His will, and He honored it. He wasted no time after I uttered, "Not my will, but Thy will be done." The Father loves eager volunteers.

Learning and maturing enough to love people unconditionally—saved and unsaved—has been the biggest opportunity of my salvation. It has also been the most challenging. We are not discipled to understand the principals of our faith around love, grace, and mercy. He said, "Therefore with loving kindness I have drawn thee" (Jeremiah 31:3), and that was true for how He drew me. It is important to be the same way with others.

If we, as individuals, will make a conscious decision to mature in our faith, we can raise the perceptions and the experiences people have with Christians. There is room for all of us to grow, and my process may look totally different from yours.

While this book can be beneficial to anyone who is Christian, it was specifically penned for un-discipled Christians and Believer's who are desparate to grow. Eighty percent of the two point two billion Believers fit that profile, which is the equivalent of 1,760,000,000 people. Our confession is what makes us Christians. What we do, and how we act, is how we communicate our Christianity to the world.

Growing is how we can change the dismal course of Christendom, and the only way to do that is to get planted. We cannot run from one place to another, never taking root, and think we are going to grow. We grow if we are planted and mature when we are watered. Remember, we need both to flourish.

As Christians, we will encounter disagreements, upsets, people making mistakes, and moral failures too. Expect it—because no one is perfect. But, it does not have to devastate us to the point that we leave the church, or don't want to have anything to do with God's system for success: the Church and His people.

Success Made Easy for Saints

Here are some simple strategies that will help us as Christians to establish strong foundations, jumpstart becoming bona fide disciples, and situating us for victory over the enemy. These few foundational tactics are presented to make us stronger in the areas where we are weak. This is the easiest way to fortify Believers individually and strengthen us collectively. If we take them on, we will insulate ourselves from being spiritually stagnate.

❏ Step One: Love Is the Key

Before we do anything, we need to learn to love God with everything in us. Every day is about love, His love. Everything we do is about love. Love is the key, and love never fails. Getting this part right is our first priority, and it will make a world of difference in everything else we do in the Kingdom.

❏ Step Two: Learn the New Testament Commandments

- **1st Commandment:** *You shall love the Lord your God with all your heart, with all your soul, and with all your mind (Matthew 22:37)*
- **2nd Commandment:** *You shall love your neighbor as yourself (Matthew 22:39)*

Most people are familiar with the Ten Commandments in the Old Testament (Exodus 20:3-17), but do we know the two in the New? As New-Testament Believers, we operate under grace, and we are directed to carry grace to the world.

The unconditional love for others, which is required of us, is obtainable if we achieve step one. If we do not walk in love for God as the foundation of our relationship with Him, what should be a love affair can easily become a nightmare.

The Father does not want kids who are unloving and mean. He wants His children to embrace His word and allow His love to pierce their hearts. We cannot give what we do not have.

If we encounter a Believer who does not have the love of God in them, and there are many, we should not judge them. Instead, we need to love them into righteous alignment and pray fervently for them. This is one of the areas we seriously lack maturity. The expression of love through us shows the world that God is alive...in us.

If we are intentional and methodical in our approach to integrate these commands into every aspect of our being, we can sabotage Satan. Our salvation makes us a legitimate threat to the enemy. However, that becomes short-lived unless we get equipped with the right tools to weather the storms, overcome the obstacles, and endure the battle.

❏ Step Three: Get Our Priorities in Order

But seek first the kingdom of God and His righteousness,
and all these things shall be added to you (Matthew 6:33)

If we are not engaged in a structured way to mature in our faith, we are likely to succumb to rituals, religion, and not a relationship. Most Christians want to grow, but they have no idea how to do it. I sure did not and neither did Neicey.

The little instruction I got was from my older brother who said, "Sis, don't stop until you get filled with the Holy Ghost." His wisdom was critical. I did exactly what he said. When Matthew cited those who hunger and thirst for righteousness shall be filled, it is true. There is no way I could do what I am doing if my brother had not planted that seed.

Matthew 6:33 was deposited in my spirit at the beginning of my fourth salvation episode. It has been a guiding light for my path and helps me to regulate my life, and manage my decisions and commitments. Today, I know the power in this Scripture, which has helped me not be susceptible to the ways of the world, the pursuit of power, titles, and so forth. All of which I was seeking before Christ. As Paul said, now I count it all as rubbish (Philippians 3:8).

When we forgo being discipled, we are in essence situating ourselves for demonic assassination. We become easy targets, because we do not know how to fight, overcome, or stand in the midst of the storm. Many Christians eventually fall, and they do not get back up. Falling or failing is not a reason to quit in Christianity, and the Scripture confirms this.

For a righteous man may fall seven times, and rise again, but the wicked shall fall by calamity (Proverbs 24:16)

❑ Step Four: Engage in Bible Boot Camp

We have to take responsibility for enrolling ourselves in Bible boot camp. This is nothing short of basic training for becoming a disciple. All of Heaven might be rejoicing that we were called out of darkness and into the marvelous light, but the enemy is already advancing in our direction to snatch us back.

It is my highest recommendation that every Believer should own a physical Bible. There is something magnificent about holding the Word of God in our bare hands. Also, reading aloud or listening to the Bible is an easy way to build our faith. It is extremely beneficial to hear the Word of God VS read the Word of God, but reading is necessary.

Faith comes by hearing, and hearing by the word of God (Romans 10:17)

When God opened my eyes to the truth, I looked at the Bible and thought, "How in the world am I going to remember all of it?" I was intimidated and overwhelmed by what seemed an impossible feat. But, the Lord comforted my heart by saying, "You get it in and I will bring it out."

So, I began reading morning, noon, and night. My Bible went everywhere I did, and it still does. God kept His word. I am amazed at how the Holy Spirit will bring to my remembrance a Scripture (John 14:26). It is virtually impossible to be effective at this if we do not learn the Word.

We must be deliberate in learning the Word of God, and that includes two things. First, we have to digest the Word regularly, and every day is best. As a newborn in the Spirit, going a day without reading is like a day without food.

Next, we have to study it. Reading and studying are not the same. We can read and not study, but we cannot study, and not read. Begin studying the Book of Romans. It is a thorough job description for disciples.

❑ Step Five: Embrace Grace

We will encounter—if we have not already—people who will burden us with condemnation as we are working out our salvation with fear and trembling (Philippians 2:12). This is a horrible experience if we ourselves do not understand grace and how it works.

Grace is when we receive the unmerited favor of God, and the bestowal of undeserved blessings. We are saved by grace. We did not earn it or work for it. It is a gift and Jesus was the perfect sacrifice so we could have it.

When we understand grace, then we will not burden ourselves, potential Believers, or our fellow brothers and sisters in Christ with unnecessary religious dogma. Unconditional love is easier to execute if we have a clear grasp on grace.

If we are operating in a religious Spirit, that means we are living under the rule of the law, operating from works, and performance, not love. The law does not allow for the application of grace. Neither does it give us room to make mistakes and correct them.

Love gives us room to fail. Love encourages the pursuit of perfection, not the goal of being perfect, which is unobtainable. Love is explained explicitly in 1 Corinthians 13, and this is the love we seek to imitate.

Love suffers long and is kind; love does not envy; love does not parade itself, is not puffed up; does not behave rudely, does not seek its own, is not pro-

voked, thinks no evil; does not rejoice in iniquity, but rejoices in the truth;
bears all things, believes all things, hopes all things, endures all things
(1 Corinthians 13:1-7)

❏ Step Six: Pursue the Holy Spirit

If we are Christians—there is only one way to be one: God's way. The constitution of our character cannot be self-governed or defined based on our personality, upbringing, or cultural background.

The hardest thing we will ever do is try to stay saved without the power of the Holy Spirit and the Word of God—they go hand-in-hand. One without the other puts us at high risk for failure.

Sometime ago, Charles E. Hackett, the Division of Home Missions National Director for a leading US denomination said, "A soul at the altar does not generate much excitement in some circles because we realize approximately 95 out of every hundred will not become integrated into the church. In fact, most of them will not return for a second visit."13 The primary reason for this is because people are not getting discipled.

Christians are not perfect people. We are people who are being perfected. If the spirit of offense is running rampant down the aisles of our hearts, I suspect we might be skewed in this area. Each one of us is on a progressive road to maturity, and clearly some are further up the street than others. However, that does not make us better.

Five years from now, Heaven forbid we are acting, thinking, and talking the same way we are now. To be effective, we have to practice self-examination, which is an area where the plot of the enemy is prospering. Most of us do not want to examine ourselves, and we do not want anyone else to do it either.

Did you know the Bible says we are accountable one to another? When was the last time you allowed someone to hold your feet to the fire about your character, motives, or your pursuits? Don't you think it is time?

If we put the Christian lifestyle into a Bible-based job description, how would you measure up? The Scripture says if we judge ourselves we will not have to be judged (1 Corinthians 11:31).

After judging ourselves, we may have to admit, that in fact, we are not doing what a Christian should be doing. If that is your position—then *congratulations*. The Bible says, the truth will make you free (John 8:32).

Now we know some of our responsibilities. We are encouraged to remain in a mode of self-examination, which is also a position of humility, a place that God favors. If we never know what is wrong, we certainly cannot fix it. We do not fear correction, we welcome it.

A righteous man who falters before the wicked is like a murky spring
and a polluted well (Proverbs 25:26)

As a final point, remember God wants all of you—and until He has all of you, does He have you at all?

DISCIPLE ME NOW: Learn – Grow – Practice - Go
The Truth

This mini assessment, which is not exhaustive, is a sampling of the lifestyle we should be living. Each item is from Scripture. As you go through it, be honest. The results are between you and God.

No matter what the outcome, do not beat yourself up or allow the enemy to make you think you are a failure. Use this knowledge as a launching pad. Work on the things you did not know or neglected. This process alone will ignite your fervor for the things of God, and strengthen your relationship with Jesus Christ. Plus, it will make you a better representative, and we need that now more than ever.

Judge Yourself **Check all that apply** **(1 Corinthians 11:31)**	A Christian/Disciple
☐ Yes ☐ No	Do you share the Good News with others who are not Christians? (1 Peter 3:9)
☐ Yes ☐ No	After you were born-again, did you change? (Romans 10:9)
☐ Yes ☐ No	Do you believe, by faith, Jesus is the Son of God, and the Messiah?

☐ Yes ☐ No		Do you have a personal prayer language?
☐ Yes ☐ No		Do you know what you should be obeying in the Word of God? (1 John 2:4)
☐ Yes ☐ No		Have you laid down your life and picked up your cross to follow Christ? (Mark 8:34)
☐ Yes ☐ No		Is your faith and trust in Jesus? (Ephesians 2:8)
☐ Yes ☐ No		Have you exchanged your will for His will?
☐ Yes ☐ No		Do you study the Word of God?
☐ Yes ☐ No		Do you have the fruit of the Spirit? (Galatians 5)
☐ Yes ☐ No		Do you subscribe to the economic giving systems of the Bible (i.e. tithing, offerings, first fruits, and alms)?
☐ Yes ☐ No		Do you love people according to how the Bible defines love in 1 Corinthians 13?
☐ Yes ☐ No		Are you willing to deny yourself (Mark 8:34)?
☐ Yes ☐ No		Do you recognize the Spirit of God is living inside of you?
☐ Yes ☐ No		Is your name written in the Book of Life (Revelation 20:11-15)?
☐ Yes ☐ No		Are you Holy? (1 Peter 1:15)
☐ Yes ☐ No		Do you know what it means to be a tabernacle not made of stone? (1 Peter 2:5)
☐ Yes ☐ No		Do you honor your body as the temple of the Holy Spirit? (1 Corinthians 6:19)
☐ Yes ☐ No		Do you believe you were created for good works? (Ephesians 2:20)
☐ Yes ☐ No		Do you know you are not your own anymore? (1 Corinthians 6:20)
☐ Yes ☐ No		Are you aware you are a royal priesthood, a holy nation? (1 Peter 2:9)
☐ Yes ☐ No		Do you accept that you are a new creation? (2 Corinthians 5:17)
☐ Yes ☐ No		Are you a light in the world? (Matthew 5:14)
☐ Yes ☐ No		Do you understand what it means to be the salt of the earth? (Matthew 5:13) Can you explain being unequally yoked? (1 Corinthians 11:1)

☐ Yes ☐ No   Have you killed the works of the flesh
                          (Galatians 5:19-21) (i.e. adultery, fornication,
                          uncleanness, lewdness, idolatry, sorcery, hatred,
                          contentions, jealousies, outbursts of wrath, selfish
                          ambitions, dissensions, heresies, envy, murders,
                          drunkenness, revelries)?

☐ Yes ☐ No   Do you understand how important it is to
                          fellowship with the Body of Christ?

☐ Yes ☐ No   Do you forgive offenses seven times
                          seventy?(Matthew 18:22)

☐ Yes ☐ No   Has God told you to do something you have not
                          done?

How do you think you did? The questions I asked are directly related to the areas in which we are faltering as representatives in God's family. Your answer to every question should be YES, except for the last one. If you answer yes to the last question it is my highest recommendation that rectifying your disobedience be a priority.

These are but a few of your responsibilities and commitments as a Christian. This is what you signed up for, but what is going on in your heart is more important. Your righteousness has to exceed the righteousness of the Scribes and the Pharisees (Matthew 5:20) who had works mastered. They were perfect in upholding the rules, but Christianity is more than what you do. It has everything to do with how you act as well. Here are the definitions for those two groups.

Scribes: leaders and teachers with authority, transcribers of religious text, legal and historical documents, learned guardian of the law and copyists.[14]

Pharisees: considered the most accurate interpreters of the law, opponents of Jesus, and protectors of the early Christians.[15] Christians are God's chosen people. It is not about Jew or Greek, male or female, slave or freeman, but it is a matter of the heart (Romans 2:28-29).

Do not be conformed to this world.

And those who are Christ's have crucified the flesh with its
passions and desires. (Galatians 5:24)

And everyone who has this hope in Him purifies himself,
just as He is pure (1 John 3:3)

The Deception

- What it takes to become a Christian is difficult. FALSE (Romans 10:9)
- Christians do not make mistakes, or do things wrong. FALSE (Proverbs 24:16)
- Christians should not socialize with non-Christians. FALSE
- How you behave as a Christian does not matter. FALSE
- Christians are superior to others. FALSE
- Non-Christians are the enemy of Christians. FALSE
- Christians are perfect. FALSE

THE PLAYERS: **THE BIBLE**
The Word of God

THE TRUTH: *All Scripture is given by inspiration of God, and is profitable for doctrine, for reproof, for correction, for instruction in righteousness, that the man of God may be complete, thoroughly equipped for every good work (2 Timothy 3:16)*

THE DECEPTION: The Word of God was authored by man

There was a time in my life when reading the Word of God was boring, monotonous, and highly intimidating. It is hard for me to say that now, but it is true. I had no idea what I was doing, how to understand it, or what it was supposed to do for me, but I read it.

Every day, when I would woke up and reached for my Bible on the nightstand. I spent about thirty minutes going through the Scriptures. Some days I pondered why I was doing it because it did not feel like I was getting anything out of it. Sadly, the thought of actually applying what I was reading was far from the forefront of my mind.

Then I would close "The Big Book" and begin my day denying the Christ I just read about, and I would be the first to wail "I'm a Christian." There was no connection to the words on those pages and how I was living my life. But, I went to church, just like millions of people.

When I experienced a genuine and undeniable spiritual conversion of being born-again, that all changed. I was not just going through the motions anymore. Something profound and life altering had occurred and I knew it. Then the Word of God came alive. It had meaning. No longer was I just reading words a distant person penned by the inspiration of God thousands of years ago.

Somehow, in the midst of my transformation, I learned that grasping the Word is a matter of the heart, not the head. When we have been touched by the undeniable hand of God, we begin to see with the eyes of our heart, not our brains (Ephesians 1:18). Ask the Lord to open the eyes of your understanding and do not be surprised if it is preceded by you being filled with His Spirit.

The Bible, which is sacred, holds the Word of God. It is the most important book we will ever read. Unfortunately, not many Christians are reading it.[16] Nothing is more important to know, outside of how much God loves us, than what He said in His Word.

Scripture is our authority on everything, and submitting to it is not optional. This is the number-one weapon we need to frustrate the plan of the enemy against our lives. The Word is to a Christian what weapons are to a soldier. Without it, we are lame ducks, sitting targets, and the enemy knows it. He will take advantage of and abuse every Christian who does not read and study.

This is what I believe Father God would say to us about the His Word:

The Scriptures are my love letter to you. These Words are a direct expression of my heart and they come straight from My throne through the vessel I choose to use to deliver them. The only role man played in what is written in the Bible is he was the vehicle.

God is the author of the Word of God and no one else can take credit. His Word is something we can always rely on to know His thoughts. He tells us what makes Him happy, and what makes Him sad.

They are His strategies for success, wisdom for relationships, methods for healing, dealing with the adversity, unity, and worship to mention a few. He talks about history, not necessarily one of my favorite subjects, but it is a necessity. He wants us to have a perspective from which to glean. His do nots are not rules—they are opportunities to soar in righteousness.

God is not controlling; His Word never dictates, it only invites—because He is our Father, and we are His children. The Bible provides the path for us to always get the best. His Word is not wishy-washy, like we might be sometimes. His Word is flawless and unchanging.

He shares how this all began and all the details in-between. As we turn the pages, we will learn His intentions and thoughts toward us. The plans He put in place for our futures, and how we can make the most of everything He said and is offering.

The more I read, the more I want to read. The more I learn, the more I understand, and the more I understand makes me realize I don't know anything. When I read the Bible, I do not get smarter, I get a little wiser.

His word causes me to thirst, and the more I thirst, the more He fills me. The more He fills me, the more I grow. The more I grow, the more I look like Him, act like Him, walk like Him, and talk like Him. Then I can do more. The more I can do, the more people are reached, helped, healed, loved, empowered, and delivered. It just gets better and better.

Hear The Word

It is written, "Man shall not live by bread alone, but by every word that proceeds from the mouth of God" (Matthew 4:4). The Word of God is sustenance and contains all the spiritual vitamins, minerals, and essentials we need to grow up in Christ. *In the beginning was the Word, and the Word was with God, and the Word was God (John 1:1).*

Every time I hear that Scripture, it reminds me of Tass Saada, a Muslim and an amazing man of hope who I had the privilege of spending time with. In his book, *Once an Arafat Man: The True Story of How a PLO Sniper Found a New Life*, he talks about how reading John 1:1 caused him to fall on his knees and blurt out *"Oh, Jesus, come into my life. Forgive me and be my Lord and Savior!"*

Out of the mouth of a man who called himself, "a Jew-hating Palestinian." After he blurted out the Word of God, supernaturally all the bitterness lodged in his heart was uprooted and dissolved. He was set free, and plopped into the Kingdom of God, murders and all, because of the living Word. The Word of God is powerful.

After years of laying hands and commanding demons to leave the minds, hearts, and bodies of Believers, one thing became very clear: the majority of them did not know the Word of God. They were not equipped to stop the vicious beatings on their lives, and because of that they suffered terribly.

Christians are experiencing devastating spiritual setbacks. Deafening personal turmoil, and the depletion of joy and mental stamina is robbing them blind. People are bankrupt by demonic assignments because they are passive to reading and knowing the Scriptures.

What should be the House of Prayer is now characterized by the moral decline of Christian character, the love of many waxing cold, and our sanctuary becoming more like a psychiatric ward. This is inevitable when Believers have no spiritual firepower in their arsenal. We can conquer darkness if we have the right tools, which begins with inhaling what God exhaled, which is His Word.

We cannot fight, in this spiritual battle, if we are Word deprived. The Enemy notices we do not use it to combat him in battle, so he forges forward to kill, steal, and destroy. Nothing that is sacred to us is important to him including our lives.

If each one of us would make it our personal responsibility to read ten minutes a day, together we can shift the spiritual current of Christianity. Reading will affect everything around us. Even though we may not fully understand what we are reading or why, it is important to do it. It will pay huge dividends and situate us to be better equipped to handle the future God wants to give us.

The Purpose Of Scripture

The purpose of Scripture, which has four components, is like having quadruplets. One is as important as the other. They are outlined in the book of Timothy.

All Scripture is given by inspiration of God, and is profitable for doctrine, for reproof, for correction, for instruction in righteousness, that the man of God may be complete, thoroughly equipped for every good work (2 Timothy 3:16-17)

Profitable definition – beneficial, useful, advantageous, and worthwhile.

- *Profitable for* **Doctrine** (policy, principals, education)
- *Profitable for* **Reproof** (criticism, reprimand, scold, admonish)
- *Profitable for* **Correction** (modification, adjustments, set right, amend)

- *Profitable for* **Instruction in Righteousness** (training, schooling, coaching, lessons)

We need each of these to be thoroughly equipped for every good work. If we are not, or have never experienced these aspects of Christian discipline, chances are…

- We may not be connected to the Body of Christ, a Christian fellowship, or a Church (Hebrews 10:25)
- We have no one holding us accountable; Jesus himself was accountable to His Father, and He was perfect; how much more do we need someone to hold us accountable?
- We have unresolved issues with leadership or maybe we are resisting authority (Hebrews 13:17)
- We may have a problem with submission; Jesus had to surrender to the pecking order and so do we (Ephesians 5:21)
- Or your heart may be hard for various reasons

If we are serious about living our best life and fulfilling our divine purpose, we have to be taught, rebuked, corrected, and trained to be honorable vessels, complete and equipped to work for God's glory. We have to evict spiritual trespassers whose mission is to hinder our victory. The only way we can do that, is if we are packing our swords—also known as the Word.

DISCIPLE ME NOW: Learn – Grow – Practice - Go
The Truth
To fortify a hedge of protection around us that is not easily infiltrated, and protect God's plan for our lives, we must…
- **Learn** the Word, and make a commitment to do it if we haven't
- **Read** the Word daily, and preferably aloud (Romans 10:17)
- **Continue** in the Word until we find freedom (John 8:31-32)
- **Hear** the Word (Luke 11:28)
- **Study** the Word (2 Timothy 2:15)

- **Pray and meditate** on the Word (Joshua 1:8)
- **Hide** the Word in our hearts (Psalm 119:11)
- **Feast** on the Word (Matthew 4:4)
- **Speak the Word** to bring things into existence (Romans 4:17)
- **Never** add to the Word (Revelation 22:18)

Things to Know about the Word of God
- Jesus is the Word of God made flesh (John 1:1)
- The Word is mighty: *For the Word of God is living and powerful, and sharper than any double-edged sword, piercing even to division of soul and spirit, and of joints and marrow, and is a discerner of the thoughts and intents of the heart (Hebrews 4:12)*
- The Word will not return void (Isaiah 55:11)
- The Word lights our path (Psalm119:105)
- We must obey the Word (James 1:22)
- The Word endures forever (Isaiah 40:8)
- The Word is always right (Psalm 33:4)

The Deception
One of the motives of the enemy regarding the Word is to stir up doubt and breed unbelief so he can discredit the Word of God. He wants us to reduce it to only being written by a man. The presence of these feelings is a breach in our relationship with Christ and we might want to rectify that mindset immediately.

Here are two ways he accomplishes his shameless endeavor. I am highlighting these two for the purpose of eliminating barriers to us coming into the fullness of God's promises.

Demonic Prophecies/No Prophecy
While demonic prophecies are not happening everywhere, it is going on enough to be addressed. Some of us are, or have been, victims of prophecies that did not come from God. Perverted prophecies are sown into our spirits to distract us, deplete our resources, frustrate our productivity, and separate us from God.

There is nothing more frustrating than trying to live out a false prophetic word. We can save ourselves a lot of time, resources, heartache, and some deep soul wounds if we have prophecies confirmed by two or three witnesses (1 Corinthians 14:29-31).

Now, on the other hand, when we treat prophets and prophesying like it is the plague, we are contributing to the demise of the Body. Without the Prophets and prophecy we are the blind leading the blind, and eventually we'll end up in a ditch. If the Scripture encourages us to desire the gift of prophecy (1 Corinthians 14:1) that means God wants us to prophesy. Everything we do must be done decent and in order, and prophecy is necessary to help grow up the sheep.

False Prophets

In the last days, there will be false prophets among us and they will prosper in their deception because people do not know the Word. They are masters at, ever-so-slightly altering, God's Word. They say things that sound good, but they are not true. Many will be led astray, but we do not have to be (Matthew 24:11).

The ultimate false prophet will be the Anti-Christ. However, before he makes his entrance, many already among us are operating in the nature of him now (1 John 2:18). They are not hard to identify, but we have to know what we are looking for.

An article titled "Ten Characteristics of the Anti-Christ According to the Bible" written by Jack Wellman said, "*The characteristics of anti-Christ's [sic]are whoever denies that Jesus is the Christ, that He is the Messiah or that He is fully God. The world has no shortage of anti-Christ's [sic]. Their characteristics are that they also deny His virgin birth, His resurrection, His living a sinless life, and that He will return again to judge the world.*"

In deliverance ministry, when a person exhibits these characteristics, we cast out the spirit of the anti-Christ. Any agreement, by anyone, Jew or Gentile, has to be addressed if you desire to be in right relationship with the Father and His Son.

The ultimate deception will be the Anti-Christ himself. He will embody a combination of behaviors and actions that will distinguish him from impersonators. He will usher in the mark of the beast, the 666, which will be directly connected to your ability to buy, sell, and access much-needed resources to survive (Revelation 13:16-18).

If we take the mark, it will separate us from God forever—and there is no going back. Once the mark makes its way into the financial system, a measure of faith will be needed to keep people from taking it. Many will succumb under pressure.

This is something you might want to study on your own, and here are a few additional markers to file away. He will attempt to support Israel, but with an ulterior motive to destroy her (Daniel 11:40-41). His ultimate goal in everything he does is to mimic the life of Christ. He will be worshiped and for us we are to worship no other. He will not be short of performing miracles either, but they will not be of God, but they will be real.

He will wow the world by dying and being resurrected (Revelation 13:3). The only difference is his resurrection is under the influence of demonic powers. Whenever we use deceptive measures or manipulation to control an outcome, we are operating in witchcraft, which is sin. It puts us outside the will of God and at serious risk of being overtaken by darkness.

Just remember, when we see the anti-Christ nature, not the person, which may be when we look in the mirror, as long as one is breathing there is hope for repentance. We are on a journey designed to go from glory to glory. The darkness has to be exposed in order for the light to consume it.

The Holy Spirit once told me, "Darkness is contagious, but righteousness has to be confessed." Do not panic, just repent and invite anyone you encounter thinking that way to do the same. And, for the sake of the Kingdom, do it in love (Galatians 6:1).

THE PLAYERS: THE CHURCH

The Individual, the Body of Christ, the Place

THE TRUTH: *Now you are the body of Christ, and members individually* (1 Corinthians 12:27), and we are the church
THE DECEPTION: The church is not relevant today

The Body of Christ (BOC) is an amazing and peculiar group of people, and we are privileged to be part of it. *Many are called, but few are chosen (Matthew 22:14),* and that is dictated by accepting or rejecting the King when He comes. Outlined are several key issues to know, be aware of, or engaged in for the purpose of being an effective and thriving member in the family.

One of my favorite Scriptures speaks directly to the current condition of the church. *We are hard-pressed on every side, yet not crushed; we are perplexed, but not in despair; persecuted, but not forsaken; struck down, but not destroyed (2 Corinthians 4:8-9).* The battle is not ours, and in the end we get the victory. But, we have to see through the eyes of faith to walk in confident assurance.

The reality of what is going on with the members does not change the truth of what God intends for His church. Every church is not in turmoil and every body of believers is not full of themselves. There are spiritual leaders who are real servants of God, who genuinely care about the sheep, and I know a few of them.

Some of our family members are in this for the long haul; we are not backsliding, or making a mockery of the Kingdom. We can breathe a sigh of relief knowing God will always have a remnant. A group of followers who will hold up the blood-stained banner, march forward in holiness and righteousness, and allow themselves to be the light at any cost.

The Bible says, *He who is in you is greater than he who is in the world (1 John 4:4).* Collectively we are a force to be reckoned with, especially when we stand in unity and move in harmony. Individually, we might not be able to leap over tall buildings in a single bound, but we can move mountains, and together we can shift nations.

There is a fierce battle raging between good and evil and we who are the church is at the center of it. The enemy is determined to pervert the concept of organized religion and he can only accomplish his pathetic goal if we allow him. The Word says, "The gates of Hell shall not prevail against it (Matthew 16:18)." We will not be beaten.

It is crucial to understand we are God's representatives. We reflect him wherever we go, in whatever we do, how we act, what we say, how we dress, and who we associate with. It does matter what people think about us if we are His. Every activity we are engaged in either adds to or takes away from the Kingdom of God.

Even something as simples as what you say is being tracked and you will give an account for everything single word (Matthew 12:36).

As Believers, we are part of a royal priesthood (1 Peter 2:9) and coheirs (Romans 8:17) with Christ, which makes us members of the most powerful family on earth. We, the family of God, and representatives of Jesus Christ, are always being watched. What people see in our behavior or attitude matters.

Once I got saved for real, I started wearing cross necklaces. One day as I was standing in line at Subway, something happened I will never forget. There was a mix up and it caused me to get mad.

Before I knew it, I whipped around to be anything but Christian, and I caught my reflection in the mirror. My cross jumped out and stopped me in my tracks. Literally, I forgot saved people do not act the way I was about to.

Now, I do not need anything on the outside to remind me of the choice I made on the inside, but my cross did make a difference. Today, I have internal controls that are far more effective.

The enemy is waging war against the congregation of God's anointed, and sometimes he is using us to do it. If we do not recognize him, we could easily become a victim, a casualty, or his perpetrator.

Our Responsibilities

We have many obligations. Some will be challenging and many are rewarding, but all are necessary. This list will help us maneuver through them with the least amount of turmoil.

- We are no longer our own; our right to be coheirs with Christ was paid for by the sacrifice that Jesus made
- We will meet people we love and adore, and we may have to leave them; there is a time and a season even for some relationships
- We will encounter difficult people; we must make a decision to love them anyhow
- Learn the tenants of the Christian faith, share them, but most of all practice them
- We are now soldiers in the Army of the Lord, with many other soldiers; we need to be trained to fight
- Coming into alignment with righteousness can be difficult for many and a messy ordeal for others; remember, it is a process, not a destination; give grace and then give some more

- Everyone in church is not our spiritual kinfolk; the wheat and the tare are living together
- Be advocates for unity in the Body
- Guard our hearts (Proverbs 4:23)

Christians are not righteous by affiliation, but by confession. And, since the Bible says know them by their fruit, make sure your fruit inspector is in good working condition.

The Church

There are the two aspects of church we should be able to distinguish. The collective group of members is the Body of Christ, which is called the Church.

But now indeed there are many members, yet one body (1 Corinthians 12:20)

The other is the building or place we go to on Sunday mornings, and that too is called the Church.

Is it not written, My house shall be called a house of prayer for all nations (Mark 11:17)

When people say negative and derogatory things about the church they are talking about the members, not the building. We can play an important role in reducing the negative dialogue by changing ourselves as members.

The Imperfect Church

It would be difficult to find one person who cannot point out something wrong with their church. No church is perfect. Once we get this, we can stop church shopping, because if we did find a perfect church, it would be flawed as soon as we got there.

Our active participation as imperfect people, in an imperfect church, is waiting. Church is the place to equip imperfect people, and it is easy to get distracted by the tornado of activities. Especially when the members are not as mature as they should be.

When I cross that threshold on Sunday mornings, my heart is focused and my actions are intentional. I remind myself to walk in love, stay in my lane, remember why I am there, do my part in excellence, as unto God, not man, be available should God want to use me, and go home. This is my strategy for succeeding in the temple.

The Pews

The church is where Believers go to fellowship, worship, and learn. The pews should be the place to equip to win souls, and not just to rest our behinds. It is time to empower the people sitting in the pews. This is imperative since the majority of our family sits in the pews, not the pulpit. If we shifted from pastors prospering to the parishioners growing, we could actually become a legitimate threat.

The P.E.W.S should be the PLACE to EQUIP to WIN SOULS

The power is in the pew where the multitudes are searching for a place of meaning, training, and activation. Instead, hope is deferred and destinies are dying. How many dreams are buried between the thirty minutes of praise and worship and the benediction?

Too many sheep are underfed, malnourished, emotionally distraught and mistreated, which hinders being able to function as God intended. They are gasping for air, as the wind of the Spirit is squeezed out. Many are succumbing to passive religious deaths as they are slowly and painfully suffocated by redundant rituals, generational rebellion and a growing resistance to truth.

If the Kingdom had a Homeland Security we would be under high alert for neglect. The Body of Christ is in critical condition and hemorrhaging. Denial is the blood thinner and dealing with the truth of our situation is the only coagulant we can administer. It is highly irresponsible if we continue to ignore weary sheep and exhausted shepherds.

The appropriate use of the pew is for it to be an equipping station or launching pad. For many, once they sit, they are sedated by pageantry, groomed as orphans, not sons, who are indebted to man instead of sold-out to Christ. No wonder millions are easy prey for the enemy. As long as the blood-bought are stuck in the pews, and not ushered into the harvest, we all suffer.

What if the solution for women aborting their babies was in the belly of someone who is stuck in the pew and is never discipled? Is it hypocritical to stand against abortion, but we are okay with millions of destinies dying every Sunday in our pews?

Where is the outrage and picket lines for that atrocity? Who will prophesy to the dry bones that march in and out every Sunday like robots? Where are the prayer warriors and intercessors for this elephant holding the elect hostage in the sanctuary? There has to be a John the Baptist waiting to exhale on them benches.

With my own eyes, I have seen a few Pauls in the making, and Esthers waiting for their moment. But, I also have seen Hamons, and Judases too. He said the wheat and the tare would grow together and He would do the separating, but we should know the difference.

Tell the Whole Truth

Can I be honest with you? My heart's cry is that we will tell ourselves the truth, or accept it when it comes, and be willing to do something about it. Faith without works is dead. Millions of Christians are failing, because we are not teaching them how to succeed.

Once upon a time, and not too many years ago, I was miserable sitting in the pews as a new Believer. It hurt my heart to see Christians interacting with one another in shallow, petty or distant ways in the name of Jesus. The love we show one another is an indication of the existence of God. How we relate and treat one another is important.

People come to church looking for answers, and it becomes difficult to stay when they do not find them. It is in the DNA of every human being to seek solutions in the church. More than once I received advice that led me to make some not so good decisions. Thank God my recovery from bad advice has been miraculous. Over time, as I stayed the course, God made the bad choices work for me, and he will do it for you too. It is one of the sweetest secrets in His Kingdom.

Now, my issues were not all because of church people, most of the bad things I did and choices I made were of my own doing. It is easy to make mistakes listening to ungodly counsel when we are spiritually immature and biblically ignorant. Before you get your feathers ruffled, it is noteworthy to say this is not everybody's experience—but the ones who can relate, and there are millions, are the ones I hope to reach.

Too many of our co-inheritors are being manipulated for personal gain. Gifts are prostituted to build shrines for dead people, and too often greed courts the rich and the famous from the pulpit. These discrepancies are a bad taste in the Spirit, and they are leaving a smell in the House of the living God that stinks like cow manure. If we fail at getting ourselves together, who is going to reach the lost if we do not?

We can bank on this: if we want to learn and grow as Believers, God will make it happen no matter what the condition of our church. The Holy Spirit is not slack in teaching us what we need to know. But, this Home Girl aint no fool. Obeying God is my insurance policy to get my inheritance, in this life and after. Not to mention, it gives me leverage to put a demand on the Word and see results.

Choosing a Church

Where I currently attend would not be my church of choice. With that being said, surprisingly it has become the first church where I found peace. Not because it is perfect. Actually, it is far from it, and neither does it meet the itemized list I keep in my head of what I want in the church I would pick.

However, now I go without fretting, being overwhelmed by the dysfunction, or sulking because I am disappointed—it does not meet my expectations. Sometimes things look crazy, but it does not mean we won't eventually prosper.

One day in Sunday school, my Pastor asked, "At what age did you come to the Lord?" The answers given were between six and twelve years old. Most of the class was well over fifty. Then I looked around and my heart sank, because week after week, several grandparents had their grandchildren with them in the adult class. Up to that point I never paid them any attention. They sat quietly unengaged in our class because there was no one to teach them.

My spirit was grieved and I knew something had to be done, but I was not sure what. Volunteering someone else probably would not have worked, even though it crossed my mind. The pastor often asked us to pray for teachers for the children and youth. Plus, he was a broken record telling everyone, "get in where you fit in," and still the laborers were few. At some point the sheep have to do more than graze.

But, I never imagined, while I was praying fervently, God would answer his prayer by using me. Through one gesture of obedience to the Holy Spirit,

I found a passion I didn't know was there, and a portal to my destiny. There are no words to explain the joy that has come from making disciples of our children.

The love children have for God is contagious. Their innocence and curiosity to learn about the Kingdom of God is a breath of fresh air. When I see them catch the revelation or practice the principals we teach, it makes my heart swell.

What I thought I would do with the adults in the church, I now do with children. It is so much easier, and way more fun. They do not pretend they know everything already. The significance and impact I believe we all seek was handed to me in the place I least expected it: in the church that was not my choice.

It is not unusual for people to choose a church based on where they think they will be able to connect and grow. What I now know is if I go to church with the mind to give, when I do, then I grow.

Give, and it will be given to you: good measure, pressed down, shaken together, and running over will be put into your bosom. For with the same measure that you use, it will be measured back to you (Luke 6:38)

If I had followed tradition, I would not have volunteered where I had no experience. You might be surprised, like I was, to learn where your gifts actually fit. Being discipled, has taught me that we go where God leads. As we mature, we do whatever God wants us to do, and we trust Him for the equipping to do it.

We also learn our inadequacy is not a hindrance, but an opportunity to put a greater demand on the Spirit to guide us. Then we know for certain it was God who did it and not us. No doubt that is what happened in this next story.

Teaching the children in my home church opened the door of my heart wider toward children and prepared me for a rare opportunity. I met a beautiful, but deeply troubled twelve-year-old girl in a group home, who expressed her love for God through indescribable pain. She told me she wanted to be baptized. When I asked her why, this is what she said, "I want all the spirits to go away so I can have the new life Jesus talked about." I think the whole world rotated on her words.

She knew her inheritance in Christ was freedom from being tormented. On the day of her baptism, I looked into those troubled little eyes and my heart exploded. When I laid her under the water and raised her up it was her new beginning—and by far, one of the best days of my life. We cried together and so did everyone else who attended.

There are people who are mad in church, or at God, or both. I was one of them, but not anymore. I cried out to God, because I knew He did not want me to be idle in the pews. It seemed my life was going nowhere and it was hard not knowing what to do. It took some time, and I went through many challenges, but He answered, and He will answer you too. I'm stronger now because I endured the test. But, you have to stay the course and ask for help as well. He will not let you down.

There is nothing wrong with desiring to do more in Christ. However, striving and competing for positions or status in the House of God is troublesome. Like many, I have strong spiritual gifts and talents, but I did not know how to use or develop them as a child of God. I was well equipped to maximize my capacity based on what I had learned in the world, but I was clueless of how that worked in the church.

Growing in the Church

Trying to mature in character and capacities in the church can feel like playing the lottery. If there is no structure in place to facilitate growth, those who need it may feel helpless. I was counting on the church to show me what to do with what God had put in me. But, that is not what happened. So, being the courageous person that I am, I stepped out in faith to exercise what God put in me, and it did not go well. Here is one example:

One day, while in Sunday morning service, when we lived in San Diego, the Spirit was high, and although I had never done this before, I felt God had given me a prophetic word for the church. We were never instructed on what to do if you were given one.

The Pastor was at the podium and I tried to find an appropriate moment to stand up and say, "Pastor I have a word for the Church." When I did, his response to me was sarcastic and dismissive.

I sat down, but I was cooking inside as my African friends would say. Eventually the pot boiled over and I grabbed my stuff in the middle of service, and walked out of the church. My attitude reeked of rejection, and it seriously needed to be adjusted, or I needed to be delivered. It was probably both.

Before I reached the door, the Holy Spirit grabbed me by the neck, and stopped me in my tracks. He spoke to my heart and said, "You are out of order." I sobered up. How could I be out of order when I know He told me to stand up and say what I said? He continued, "Your job is to do what I tell you." Then He said, "It is my job to deal with those who do not respond to my messengers properly when I send them, not yours."

The Holy Spirit was right. There was nothing else to be said, and I apologized to God. Then I turned around and marched back to my seat, put my jacket and purse down, and started clapping like I never missed a beat. No doubt, the people in service had to be thinking, "Did she forget her medication?"

When service was over, I went to the Pastor and apologized for my disrespectful behavior. The apology was not for trying to release a prophetic word, but for leaving when he did not receive that I was sent by God. I did my part by confessing and apologizing, and He will have to give an account for his.

We also have to accept that the order of the church is the responsibility of the Pastor or leader. We are to submit to their decisions even when we do not like them. It is within their discretion to use our gifts or not, but it is never appropriate to neglect, abuse, or minimize the sheep. We may have to tarry a while before we see this one come to pass.

Christians are weary in the church, because their gifts are not being developed or used. You might be one of them, and I know the feeling. Do not faint; stay the course. Acknowledge God in everything you do and He will direct your steps (Proverbs 3:6).

Millions do time in the hope-deferred position, like my sister and I, wanting to be discipled, and desperately needing encouragement. Are you pondering the question, "When is it my turn?"Most Christians do not realize to be used in the harvest is not contingent upon our church, but our hearts. Waiting for a position in our church is not the path to our promise.

There is a time and a season for every gift, including yours (Ecclesiastes 3). Be patient and wait for it. Your destiny is not in the hands of man. In the interim, focus on mastering the fruit of the Spirit so when your gift is released it comes forth from good ground. Your brothers and sisters in Christ will give you ample opportunity to practice.

God has given us instructions to occupy until He comes (Luke 19:13), which can be done without being a rebel or usurping the spiritual authority of our religious institutions. The only prerequisite to action is to be filled with the Promise. Once we have that, the Bible says we are ready to go. But, for those who don't know what to do—or who are a bit more timid—I have specifically outlined activations in "The Commissioning" section of this book.

Going to Church

Not long ago I ministered to a dear sister in the faith who was in a cycle of disappointment about her church. Sound familiar? My heart empathized with her because I know what it feels like to be in that place, and maybe you do too. Also, we can be happy with where we go to services, but that doesn't mean we are getting what God intended for us to have. *Satisfied* does not equal *spiritually successful*, or *righteously aligned*.

First, everything broken—or what we think is broken in our churches—is not necessarily for us to fix. Second, sometimes we encounter things to teach us how to endure. Other times God brings it to our attention so we can pray. Third, if there are issues or people appearing to be working against us, remember all things are going to work together for your good, as God promised (Romans 8:28). That is, if we keep ourselves in righteous alignment through the process. We are not suffering for righteousness' sake, unless we are operating righteously.

Sometimes people use deception, manipulation, and/or intimidation to get others to do what they want. In the Kingdom, these are not authorized nor endorsed practices. Trying to control others is not proper church etiquette either. Truth must always be the leader of the pack.

Church Attendance

Did you know God's family is not growing? We are losing more siblings than we are gaining. Many times when a church is experiencing growth, in reality they have only gained members another church lost. What we want is fresh converts so the lineage of Christ itself is growing.

The article "Statistics and Reasons for Church Decline", projected by 2025 only fifteen percent of the population will be in church on a regular basis and that number will significantly decline by 2050 to about eleven to twelve percent.[17] Although thousands of people are converting everyday to Christianity, those abandoning the faith are significant. Even though it is scriptural that in the last days there will be a great falling away, it should not be because we are not doing our part.

We might want to commune with ourselves about our evangelistic contribution to the Body. Do we witness, share our testimonies, or tell lost souls the Good News that they do not have to remain lost? Chances are—we don't. Overall, we are not good at sharing the gospel. Mostly, because nobody ever taught us, but we can learn. The priority of sharing the Good News about Jesus has taken a back seat to religious rituals, rhetoric, and complacency.

This reminds me of the first church I attended in San Diego. There was a guy we called the Screaming Deacon. His passion for God and witnessing was electrifying, and I wanted the freedom of expressing my faith like him. His love for God was contagious.

Every time he spoke, I sat in awe of his enthusiasm and fire. Unbeknownst to me I joined the church right before its demise. In the midst of the chaos, God did not stop moving. As it crashed to the ground, the spiritual atmosphere was still loaded with goodies.

The leaders were bickering and I was gleaning how to war in the spirit. Individuals were falling and I was learning how to stand. Our Kingdom family was being scattered, and in the midst, God was telling me, "Do not let go." Mantles were dropping, and I was picking them up.

After all the favored people left, I got to practice being in leadership. Sometimes when we think nothing is happening, something is. My tank was being filled with tools and capacities that today I know came from a church in turmoil. It worked for my good.

Growth is a given in the midst of things going haywire. We get the chance to work with what we have or see what we don't. Both are opportunities to learn if we look at it with that perspective. Do not panic or quit just because everybody else is. That may not be God's plan for you.

Have you ever asked yourself why we go to church? There is no doubt some of our pastors are asking the same question. Are we going because of tradition? I once did. Maybe we go because we want to please God. We could be like my sister Neicey—we want more, so we go, but we do not know how to get it.

The ritual of Church Going looks like this. We see it every Sunday. People park in the same spot, if they can. We sit in the same row, because if we sit in the seat consummated weekly by someone else's behind, we might become a victim of a Believer gone bad.

We say hello to a few people, and wait without protest for the routine. Then comes the music and sometimes it is really good, and other times we appreciate the effort. The lights are turned down in the sanctuary and everyone is focused on the worship team, the choir, or whomever is the designated performer for the day. Why do we turn the lights off?

Next, it is time to give. Have we made peace with the practice of letting go of the dough? Or, are we in the count with the majority? Remember, the path to destruction is wide and many go there. Yes, giving in the church has been corrupted and abused in many ways, but that does not negate that as Christians we are to give to God's house.

Chances are we have not been taught the importance of giving, or how giving is the path to provision and miracles. Since long before I really surrendered my life to Christ, my checkbook was lined up with the highly talked about call to tithe, and it has served me well.

Giving is an act of obedience, not a gesture of generosity. Once we decide to obey, and obedience is a decision—not a feeling—giving is easy. Gladly, I give ten percent of everything that comes into my hands, and all seven promises associated with tithing have been my portion, and then some. Did you know, tithing is the only time God allows you to challenge Him to do what He said? Who would miss the opportunity to try God? Listen to what He said:

"Bring all the tithes into the storehouse, that there may be food in My house, And try Me now in this," says the Lord of hosts, "If I will not open for you the windows of heaven And pour out for you such blessing that there will not be room enough to receive it. "And I will rebuke the devourer for your sakes, So that he will not destroy the fruit of your ground, nor shall the vine fail to bear fruit for you in the field," says the Lord of hosts; "And all nations will call you blessed, for you will be a delightful land," says the Lord of hosts (Malachi 3:10-12)

But, for those of us who are not persuaded about tithing, try this. As born-again Believers, our lives are no longer our own—and neither are our talents, time, houses, cars, or money. We are now stewards for the benefit of the Kingdom, and everything we have now belongs to God. Might I engage you in developing your relationship with the Father to this affect? He wants to use everything we have for His glory, even your money.

Forsake Not the Fellowship

If we want to keep things lined up biblically, the Word says do not forsake assembling with the brethren (Hebrews 10:25). Bedside Baptist, Cable C.O.G.I.C., or Podcast Presbyterian should never be substituted for being in direct contact with His Body.

For those of you who are not physically able to go to church, then we the church should be coming to you. How easy would it be to deploy teams of two to visit the sick, shut-in and hospitalized?

Now, on the other hand, some people are never going to make it through the doors of the church. This does not mean they will not be sitting next to us inside the pearly gates. Are we prepared to shift our thinking from going to church to how to "BE" the church wherever we go?

The Bad

As a whole, we have taken a beating, but not all of our suffering and persecution has been for righteousness. Even though we are guilty of a lot, His blood will cover the multitude of our discretions. Now, do not take that as an excuse to act unbecoming, or a permission slip to misbehave. The Father knows our hearts, and grace is not a crutch.

Every day thousands join the church, but most never cross over to becoming active members. Some thought they converted, but never really did. Others are wounded and did convert, but never got discipled. Most are released into the fold ill prepared for battle, bleeding, and compromised. This is problematic, especially when those confessing born-again rights are still infested with worldly rodents, carnal lice, and mental bed bugs.

Anyone who comes in contact with them are at risk of being wounded by friendly fire, which is fueling the 2.7 million Believers annually falling away into inactivity, in the United States alone.[18] This epidemic is a spiritual cancer affecting the Body worldwide. We all must submit to biblical doctrine and not personal agendas.

Eighty percent of 2.2 billion Christians have not been introduced to the mandate in Matthew 28:19-20, which is *to make disciples*. Uninformed Believers are having more temper tantrums than a kindergarten classroom. But, this can be fixed. The world, now more than ever, needs us to grow up, leaders included.

Also, in the event you have been intimidated by a Believer who has been in the pews for years, know this: longevity is not the equivalent of maturity. Decades in the church does not mean you have grown. Maturity is demonstrated in our capacity to repent and humble ourselves, stand under the pressure, deal with conflict, say we're sorry, and walk in the fruit of the spirit (i.e. love, joy, peace, longsuffering, kindness, goodness, faithfulness, gentleness, and self-control; Galatians 5:22-23a). Some people spend a lifetime in church and they are still bitter, unforgiving, and immature.

No one needs a title to minister to the people in their family, or on their job, in the grocery story, or at the movies. No license is required to love unconditionally. We are free to grace the podium in the highways or byways any day of the week. Jesus said the greatest amongst us are the servants. Have you noticed there are no ordinations services for that position?

There are billions of people waiting to hear the Good News, to be given a prophetic word that is undeniably God, or desperate to experience healing by His love. Our passion should not be getting into the pulpit, but ministering to the people.

Who is willing to rush to the platforms in prisons or meet the needs of the poor? Where are the Christians to help the widows, the grandparents raising their grandchildren, and tend to the orphans?

I know from talking to them that many of the Believers behind bars are wondering if they have been forgotten. The places we should be reaching, which are outside the walls of the church, those stages remain empty of vessels available and eager to serve those who need Him most.

The Ugly

This is a war with casualties, but most Christians do not see it that way. Salvation is the door to the battle brewing against Believers. These are the last days and the deception and persecution of the past is going to get worse. Do not let your ears be tickled by false facts about the future. Your Bible spells out exactly what is going to happen. All you have to do is read 2 Timothy 3:1-7 which says:

But know this, that in the last days perilous times will come: For men will be…

❑ *lovers of themselves*
❑ *lovers of money*
❑ *boasters*
❑ *proud*
❑ *blasphemers*
❑ *disobedient to parents*
❑ *unthankful*
❑ *unholy*
❑ *unloving*
❑ *unforgiving*
❑ *slanderers*
❑ *without self-control*
❑ *brutal*
❑ *despisers of good*
❑ *traitors*
❑ *headstrong*
❑ *haughty*
❑ *lovers of pleasure rather than lovers of God*
❑ *having a form of godliness but denying its power*

And from such people turn away! For of this sort are those who creep into households and make captives of gullible women loaded down with sins, led away by various lusts, always learning and never able to come to the knowledge of the truth (2 Timothy 3:1-7)

Do a self-inventory. Also, look around at some of the fruit we have been munching on or even dispensing ourselves. If you look closer can you see hair, teeth, or eyes hiding? It might not be fruit after all, at least not good fruit. We can be deceived by both people and angels (2 Corinthians 11:14).

You will know them by their fruits. Do men gather grapes from thornbushes or figs from thistles? Even so, every good tree bears good fruit, but a bad tree bears bad fruit. A good tree cannot bear bad fruit, nor can a bad tree bear good fruit. Every tree that does not bear good fruit is cut down and thrown into the fire. Therefore by their fruits you will know them (Matthew 7:16-20)

Unfortunately, there is a growing surge of people who do not want anything to do with Christians, because their lives are inconsistent with their faith. Society is changing toward us and it is not for the better. It was reported in 2015 that there was more persecution against Christians than any other time. We are seeing an increase in people confessing Christianity in the face of dire circumstances, and for some it is costing them their lives.

If we are Christians, we have to believe the Bible and everything in it. This issue is fueling a firestorm of backlash against Christianity. Picking and choosing what we are comfortable believing is not an option. Christianity is not a democracy.

Church Leadership

Before we discuss church leadership, let me say this. First, I would like to apologize to each of you who may have experienced something, disturbing, inappropriate, mean, un-Christlike, and just wrong, at the hands of a spiritual leader in the Body of Christ. They are not perfect, but neither are you. This can be a hard lesson to learn, and that I speak from experience, but nevertheless we must learn it. Forgiveness is a sure path to spiritual freedom.

Some Know Not What They Do

As a leader myself, I have made many mistakes and I am grateful when the people whom I hurt forgave me. It is the right thing to do, and now it is time for you to do it too. Forgiveness is liberating and it is one of the quickest ways to overcome the plot of the enemy.

God wants you to release any leader who has hurt you. This directive is not up for discussion, because we have to forgive to be forgiven (Matthew 6:14). Un-forgiveness circumvents spiritual progress and it puts us in a displeasing place with God. To move forward, we have to submit to the Word of God on forgiveness.

Yes, you can do it. Say this simple prayer:

Father I forgive (offender's name), and (offender's name), and (offender's name)… for what they did to me. I also ask you to forgive me for holding bitter feelings in my heart toward them.

Today, by faith, I release them from any wrong doing, and I send them the grace I want for myself. I honor your Word to love my enemies, to bless those who curse me, to do good to those who hate me, and pray for those who use and persecute me (Matthew 5:44).

Heal my heart and release the wounds from my soul. I command any spirits that came in through the door of un-forgiveness to go. (Take another deep breath and blow out). *You are no longer welcome in this temple and you must leave now. This I do by faith, in the name of Jesus. Amen.*

Now, every time you think of that person, take control/authority over any negative thoughts, cast them down and speak blessings over the person. Give yourself permission to be free, again, and again, and again.

If you are reading this book and you are a leader in the House of God or you desire to be one, the season dictates we must equip and deploy the Saints. The church is spiritually constipated. Too many people are on inside, and not enough are working the harvest on the outside. Our goal is not to entertain one another. You, as a leader, can single-handily change the course of Christendom if you start deploying the sheep.

Overall, it is safe to say that most of our church leaders are sincere individuals who genuinely want to see the Body of Christ flourish. On the other hand, I have heard, observed, and been a victim of poor spiritual leadership in the church. Now, while this subject certainly warrants discussing, I want to focus on the individual, and how we interact with our church leaders. This section alone, if grasped righteously, can save us deep hurt and frustration, and catapult us into unprecedented progress.

If you hold an offense toward a leader, ask God to forgive you for letting the sun go down on your wrath (Ephesians 4:26). We are instructed not to carry our grievances to bed and certainly not for months or years. At some point, we are all guilty of doing this; just remember, He said you can be angry, but do not sin. If you sin, repent.

The leadership in the Kingdom of God needs our submission, and participation. They cannot do it alone, even though many try. Our prayers and continued intercession for them and how they fulfill their assignment is critical to their future and/or success. Often, they are attacked more than we are. Here are five simple ways to align with God and support church leaders:

1. Pray for them and their families
2. Encourage them often
3. Learn their vision, share it with others, and contribute to it

4. Squash gossip about your leaders and do not allow people to dump their grievances on you about your leaders
5. Find your place in their vision, serve as unto God and encourage those around you to do the same
6. Become one

Of course, this is not everything we can do, but it is a start. If we do not support our leaders, or cannot submit to their leadership, then we might want to find a leader we can support. The Scripture is very specific about how we are to conduct ourselves with spiritual authorities, and complaining about our leaders, which I have been guilty of, is not one of them.

Obey those who rule over you, and be submissive, for they watch out for your souls, as those who must give account. Let them do so with joy and not with grief, for that would be unprofitable for you(Hebrews 13:17)

If we find ourselves subjected to an abusive leader, in any form, exposing is not the same as complaining. If we want to keep the sheep safe all leaders should be accountable to someone, as well as unto the Lord.

Church structure is necessary, but it can also be tricky and flawed, but we still have to honor it. Connect with your leader. Remember, there is only one of them, and many of us, so do not take it personal they have not come to find you. The leader may not be your direct line of communication, but whomever he/she designates, which might be a care pastor, cell group leader, or assistant, be sure to meet them.

If the structure is dysfunctional and God positions you to address it, do so without being disruptive, a know-it-all, or disrespectful. Your job is never to tell your spiritual leader what he or she should do, but you can discuss or suggest. And, be sure to pray for wisdom and divine timing. Also, how you say something can be just as important as what you say, so choose your words.

No matter how our leaders act, we have a responsibility to honor and respect them. Maturing comes in the face of adversity, discomfort, and disappointment. He used my leader's shortcomings to expose mine. When I let Him, He perfected me in His image through whatever I was going through. But, I had to lay down my pride and that was hard. Sometimes it was excruciating, but only because my flesh was not dead.

We must make sure we are praying for our leaders and those throughout the Body to lead God's people with wisdom, reverence, and humility—especially if we see they are not. Our prayers matter and can make a difference.

Learning submission to authority is right up there with breathing. If we cannot or will not submit to our leaders, whom we can see, it will be difficult for us to submit to God, whom we cannot see (1 John 4:20). I am not talking about blind obedience, but prayerful compliance, to the people who give a report to the Father about us. We risk being chastened when we go against the grain.

Moral failure of a leader is not necessarily a reason to leave our churches. They have as much right to confess and repent as we do. They are under the same dispensation of grace as we are. Leaders are not immune to the wicked darts of the enemy, and his traps to kill, steal, and destroy. Actually, they are more susceptible to his vicious attacks because if he can get them, it's a good chance he'll be able to take us down too.

Now do not get it twisted; I would never condone moral perversion, including with leaders. The problem is not the falling, but what we do after the fall. Father gives us clear instructions on how to handle it when someone does and it is important to know.

Brethren, if a man is overtaken in any trespass, you who are spiritual restore such a one in a spirit of gentleness, considering yourself lest you also be tempted. Bear one another's burdens, and so fulfill the law of Christ (Galatians 6:1-2)

Now, there are some people in leadership whose motives are evil, unholy, and flat out deceptive. They are wolves in sheep's clothing (Matthew 7:15), with an agenda. I believe individuals of this nature are sometimes leading the sheep...astray. It had to be said. Be sure to watch at all times, and pray without ceasing (Ephesians 6:18).

Leaders with issues of rejection and abandonment that are not resolved are likely to inflict more wounds on their sheep. This is one reason why Believers are moving to other sections of the vineyard. Shifting sheep is not something we can control, and people should not be mistreated because they decide to go to another church. Also, for the record, nowhere in the Bible does it say you

will stay in the same church for the rest of your born-again life. There are consequences for bad Believer behavior and that goes for leaders too.

> *Be diligent to know the state of your flocks, And attend to your herds*
> *(Proverbs 27:23)*

Leaving the Church

There are a couple of things to consider as a member of the Church body.
The Scriptures say there will be a great falling away. Be not surprised that the
Body of Christ is on the decline.

> *Now the Spirit expressly says that in latter times some will depart from the*
> *faith, giving heed to deceiving spirits and doctrines of demons, speaking lies*
> *in hypocrisy, having their own conscience seared with a hot iron*
> *(1 Timothy 4:1-2)*

There is never a good reason to separate from the Body of Christ, but
there can be motivating causes for us to leave our own church. It is important
how we leave. Separating from the fellowship can be an open door to serious
demonic attacks. Especially if we leave because of an offense.

If this is true, and you left the flock because of church hurt, please read
one of my favorite books: *The Bait of Satan: Your Response Determines Your
Future* by John Bevere. It will help you understand how to not allow offense
to rule in your emotions.

The bitter battles between Believers are killing our reputation. Make a
decision to be a peacemaker at all costs, for with it comes a promise, that you
will be called the sons of God (Matthew 5:9).

Also, we should never leave a church because we discover they have issues. We all have issues. Only leave when God instructs us to do so and not a
minute before. It is possible we could miss our blessing and the opportunity to
grow through the very thing we are trying to avoid.

The church has to share the good news of Jesus Christ and proclaim it to
the entire world before the end will come (Matthew 24:14). The only way we
can accomplish this goal is if the church is functioning properly, and to do
this we all must do our part. In Ephesians 4:11-16, which you should read for

yourself, it gives us a clear strategy of how to equip the saints. It goes on to tell us how we can mature and not continue to be stuck drinking milk.

As a final point, the Bible says in James 1:8, *a double-minded man is unstable in all his ways.* Christians who drink the Kool-Aid of deception are easily swayed by what looks right, sounds good, and makes them feel happy. Be careful that you are not being led astray.

Nones and Dones are two words that describe people who are leaving the church. Both have little tolerance for being affiliated with unproductive, unorganized, and irrelevant religion. But, no matter how bad we have jacked up God's beautiful institution of righteousness called the Church, it is worth the fight to stay. Wisdom says do not let anyone deter us from what God deems as necessary and good.

DISCIPLE ME NOW: Learn – Grow – Practice - Go
The Truth
Here are a few reasons we go to church:

- To learn how to become disciples.
- It's a great place to practice unconditional love (1 John 4:11)
- We learn how to walk in unity (Ephesians 4:25)
- To enjoy corporate worship (Psalm 91:2)
- To get equipped to evangelize (Romans 1:16)
- Learn what our spiritual gifts are and practice using them (1 Corinthians 12:4-11)
- Grow in faith by hearing the Word of God (Romans 10:14)

The Deception
- Every church is led by one of God's children—FALSE
- Going to church makes a person a Christian—FALSE
- Many of the religious rituals performed in church are biblically necessary—FALSE
- There are no consequences for Shepherds who hurt or allow wounding to the sheep—FALSE—*Shepherd the flock of God which is among you, serving as overseers, not by compulsion but willingly, not for*

dishonest gain but eagerly; nor as being lords over those entrusted to you, but being examples to the flock; and when the Chief Shepherd appears, you will receive the crown of glory that does not fade away (1 Peter 5:2-4)

THE PLAYERS: **THE HOLY SPIRIT**

The Spirit of God

THE TRUTH: *But the Helper, the Holy Spirit, whom the Father will send in My name, He will teach you all things, and bring to your remembrance all things that I said to you (*John 14:26*)*

THE DECEPTION: You do not need the Holy Spirit

The Holy Spirit is a very weighty subject. He is the difference between Believers who grow and those who do not. Our relationship with Christ and effectiveness in ministry has everything to do with us knowing who the Holy Spirit is, what He does, why we need Him, and how to get filled. We cannot be easily overthrown, compromised, or hindered when we are spirit-filled, and can identify if we are hosting or being seduced by a counterfeit.

Since I am not interested in ending the life of more trees unnecessarily, let me be brief with what the Bible recommends and reinforces on this topic. Seeking God for the infilling of the Holy Spirit with the evidence of your heavenly language is a directive. The Holy Spirit is a must have, He is not *optional*. We are advised not to do the work of the ministry without Him. If you are already full steam ahead, and do not have the Holy Spirit, heed the Word and tarry until the Promise comes (Acts 1:4).

Holy Spirit

The Holy Spirit is one of the three parts of the Godhead, which includes God and Jesus. Other names for the Holy Spirit are the Holy Ghost, the Comforter, and Teacher. The Holy Spirit is a person, not a thing. We build a relationship with the Holy Spirit the same way we do with the Father and His Son. Did you know that?

Talking about the Holy Spirit reminds me of the first break-up in ministry I went through. For a minute, I was part of a dynamic group of women ministers interested in working outside the walls of the church. But, before we could get our feet off the ground, we ran into a major conflict having to do with the Holy Spirit.

The woman leading the ministry, who is a lovely sister in the faith, wanted to have church in the park. Her vision was to minister to pimps, prostitutes, and the homeless. It was a really noble idea.

As a baby Christian at the time, I was excited to do anything I could to share the Good News. But, I wasn't crazy! It does not take the Holy Spirit to tell me not to lure a whore from a pimp without the security of the Holy Spirit. Wisdom says do not start searching for souls until you do.

Ignorant desire isn't good, rushing feet make mistakes
(Proverbs 19:2 CEB)

First things first people. She was compelled to do it anyhow, which is fine. But, as far as I was concerned, she would be stealing from pimps without me. It is not safe to evangelize without the Holy Spirit.

You would not believe how many people we do deliverance on at the House of Healing because they picked up transfer spirits from witnessing without the Witness. Ignorance can cost you your life. Plus, we get no jewels in our crown for a lack of common sense.

Christians must be Spirit baptized, which is how we are empowered to minister on God's behalf. We need the supernatural power that comes from the Holy Spirit (Acts 1:8). Do not let anyone make you think being Spirit-filled is optional. It is not. When someone is against us getting spirit filled or speaking in tongues, they are in conflict with the Word of God, not us.

It is highly possible we are being set up to fail, and that could be hazardous to our spiritual health. We must regard them with caution. The enemy has no problem planting his cohorts in our midst with their hidden agendas. People who are anti- Holy Spirit may fit into one of the following categories:
1. They are afraid (fear spirit) of the unknown
2. They do not know, understand, or have wrongly interpreted the Scriptures

3. They are an undercover wolf in sheep's clothing and want to keep us dis-
empowered

We can never go wrong if we will trust God and His Word. Use extreme
caution when taking spiritual advice from someone who is not born-again or
Spirit-filled. The Scriptures are clear. Jesus told the disciples to wait for the
promise of the Holy Spirit, before they go out and act in His name. It is a pre-
requisite. If the disciples of His day needed it, what makes us think it does not
apply to us now? We cannot sign up for English 201 in college until we have
successfully completed English 101.

Talking about the Holy Spirit and speaking in tongues among Believers is
as hot a topic as when people discuss politics, abortion, or same-sex marriage.
It causes the spirit of division to rear its ugly head. God is not the author of
confusion; allow people to have their opinions until God opens the eyes of
their heart.

We have to determine not to become distracted and lured into a vicious
assault on our portion from the King. It is important not to debate, justify, or
defend as the battle is not ours (2 Chronicles 20:15). Meet the conflict with
love and compassion. Then pray for the person to get what you want or already
enjoy. Listen, you might be the only intercessor they will ever have. In the
interim, keep these Scriptures in mind:

Now I urge you, brethren, note those who cause divisions and offenses, con-
trary to the doctrine which you learned, and avoid them. For those who are
such do not serve our Lord Jesus Christ, but their own belly, and by smooth
words and flattering speech deceive the hearts of the simple
(Romans 16:17-18)

The Holy Spirit is the second baptism, water is the first, and we need them
both (Acts 1:5). There are many facets to this necessary and exhilarating gift
we will want to study, but here are a few worth mentioning now:
- With the Holy Spirit, we can know all things (1 John 2:27)
- He teaches (John 14:26)
- Intercedes for us in prayer (Romans 8:27)
- Convicts us of sin (John 16:8)
- Helps us in our weaknesses (Romans 8:26)

Also, through the power of the Holy Spirit, we are able to do what is supernatural in the natural. For example, I got a call one evening from a woman whose husband had stage-four cancer. He was in a lot of pain and she was desperate for help.

I prayed for the pain to stop so he could rest, and it happened. Pain is a spirit we have authority over when we have the Holy Spirit. Neither is this power restricted by distance because God is omnipresent (Proverbs 15:3). He wants us to use the power He has given us.

The Pastor had the best pain medication a cancer patient can get, and it did nothing. But, the power of the Holy Spirit moved on him and he slept peaceful and pain-free all night. Now, that was a miracle.

When we feel convicted in our hearts for doing something that goes against the will of God, that is an impression from the Holy Spirit (John 16:8). The manifestations of the Holy Spirit include, but are not limited to, the ability to witness, heal the sick, and cast out demons—something we all should be doing. Look around, there has to be at least one person you know who could use this spiritual service.

This gift is ours for the asking and we receive it by faith (Luke 11:13). Or, we can have a Believer lay hands on us to get it (Acts 8:17). Once we acknowledge we can do nothing of ourselves, we are in the perfect spiritual position to be baptized in fire. If you think you can handle salvation without it, my prayer is that mercy will meet you when you fall (Proverbs 16:18). But when you get it, you will know for sure, you got it.

There are so many wonderful things to learn about the Holy Spirit, but some of them we have to experience. It is not the will of God for us to live vicariously through anyone else. He has a portion with our name on it. It is time for us to get what is rightfully ours.

A Testimony of Tongues

One of the most powerful experiences in my life was the day I got filled with the Holy Spirit. At the same time I also received my heavenly language, which is called *Glossa* in Greek. Back then, I did not know using my Spirit language was a way to supernaturally strengthen my then fragile inner man (Ephesians 3:16). I learned quickly how important it is to be Spirit-filled.

Getting spirit baptized happened at the conclusion of my first three-day fast without food, and only water. I was excited for several reasons. First, I never imagined I could go that long without eating. You will be surprised by what you can do once you are spirit-filled.

I was fasting for direction on a marriage proposal and needed a clear answer on which way God wanted me to go. When I got home from church, I went upstairs to my bedroom, and began to pray to conclude my fast.

Before I knew it, the presence of the Holy Spirit had filled the room, and an undeniable sensation erupted from my mouth. My *Glossa* gloriously burst forth non-stop for the next thirty minutes. A language I did not understand eagerly rolled off my lips and kissed my ears. My experience was profound, but for you it may look different.

The presence of the Holy Spirit was so strong I had to call somebody and tell them what was happening. When my friend answered the phone, I tried to talk, and it sounded like English was my second language. I could not complete a sentence without rivers of living water cascading over every syllable.

That day is etched on the wall of my mind. Three days later, the man who asked me to marry him a week earlier, died suddenly overseas. The news sent me into a tailspin. There was nothing to stop the mental and emotional shockwaves. I could not hold on to my mind; no matter how hard I tried, it kept slipping away. My heart exploded into a thousand pieces.

Ironically, I was fasting about whether I should marry him, and instead of getting a husband, God filled me with His Spirit. It did not seem fair at the time. But, there is no doubt having the Holy Spirit, and using my *Glossa* for a few days, saved me from going over the edge. It did not take long to learn who kept me in my darkest hour.

Many converts backslide because they were never filled with the Holy Spirit, which is what happened to me the first, second, and third time I confessed Christ as my Savior. Going to church does not mean we are Spirit-filled, and neither does being on the deacon board, or holding a leadership position. Heck, as a matter of fact it is possible your Pastor may not be Spirit-filled. Sitting in the pew for decades does not give us any clout either. God wants His elect to be led by the Spirit and not out of the flesh—and without question, there is a difference.

Glossa **Is Our Gift**

Speaking in tongues is probably one of the most underutilized gifts in the Kingdom of God. I could not imagine doing ministry or witnessing without it.

For me, that would be torture. *Glossa* is a gift I treasure, and I did not have to pay Rosetta Stone a couple hundred dollars to get it. It is free for the asking.

Your special language is so unique only God can understand or interpret it (1 Corinthians 14:2). The enemy can understand our natural language, but he cannot decipher our tongues. It sounds unfamiliar at first, but God recognizes every syllable because the dialect is driven by Him through the power of the Holy Spirit inside of us. You have to admit that is pretty darn awesome.

Some people think speaking in tongues is demonic, but do not be alarmed. They accused Jesus of healing by means of Beelzebub, another name for the enemy (Luke 11:15). This line of thinking is an attempt to manipulate Believers from wanting their gift and experiencing the benefits that go along with it. The enemy knows if Christians get equipped with their *Glossa* he will have to take a back seat. So, he plants distorted seeds—explosive lies—and pedals unbelief to those who are willing to listen.

My oldest brother is the one who impressed upon me to pursue God to be spirit-filled. In his appeal, there was an urgency he attempted to convey, but I had no idea why. All I knew, was if God had a gift for me, I would not stop until it was mine. I wanted it desperately, and He gave it to me with the same amount of fire I pursued it.

He does not give it to us because it is written. We get it because of our earnest desire to have it. Ask and you shall receive, and persist until you do. It is well worth it. Now, if you have been at this for a while, do not give up. You are closer than you think. Sometimes we have to dislodge a barrier to release it. Ask the Holy Spirit to reveal any hindrance, and before you know it, you will be speaking in tongues too.

People who do not speak in a heavenly language are usually the ones who fuel the firestorm of complaints. If I knew then, what I know now, I would have flipped the script and laid hands on them until I heard Holy utterances, instead of religious squawking. You cannot imagine how many times people get viciously assaulted by the virgin *glossalalias*. If you do not want your gift, do not be mean because someone else does.

Now, that does not negate there are times when we tongue-talkers are completely out of order with our spiritual power tool. Yep, I am confessing for those of us who will not. I am so sorry to anyone I confused with my immaturity by using my tongues inappropriately. Your tongues are for private prayer, not to be publically paraded, unless they are being interpreted (1 Corinthians 12:10).

But, misuse of it is not an excuse to eliminate or discourage what God has graciously provided for His little ones. Abuse usually stems from a lack of training, and sometimes rebellion. Whichever it is, we only need to handle it accordingly, and continue on.

Are you afraid to speak in tongues? I ask because two things usually stop people from receiving the gift of *Glossa*: fear and ignorance, and both can be overcome. Fear is a spirit and it should be handled scripturally. God said, *"I have not given you a spirit of fear (2 Timothy 1:7)"*, so it comes from the enemy. Anything the enemy sends we have the power and authority to remove.

We can command fear to let go of us. Or, we can bind it in the name of Jesus, which hinders its capacity to operate. Do both or whatever else it takes. Sometimes spirits are stubborn, but do not be discouraged. This process may require repeating. We do not have to be subjected to a spirit of fear in any area of our lives.

Now, ignorance is something totally different. Overcoming it can be a challenge or as easy as renewing our minds (Romans 12:2). The first order of business is for us to know we are not alone in having it or not having it. Here are a few Scriptures to study and meditate on that will jumpstart the renewal of your mind:

- Read all of 1 Corinthians 14 and the supplemental Scriptures to deepen your understanding
- There are two types of tongues; one is for personal prayer which is used in private (1 Corinthians 14:2), and the other is for interpretation, which is for public use (1 Corinthians 14:27-28)
- Edify yourself by speaking in tongues (1 Corinthians 14:4); do this whenever you feel weak, need strength to endure, overcome, or stand
- A Spirit-filled Believer can lay hands on you to facilitate you being baptized in the Holy Spirit and to speak in your *Glossa* (Acts 19:6)
- The Spirit of God is the one who fills you with the utterances to speak in tongues (Acts 2:4)

Once you start speaking in tongues, you can do it again and again. You only have to open your mouth and speak just like you do in the natural. The only difference is the Holy Spirit is giving you the utterances. The language is not coming from your mind.

In an article in Charisma News titled "Stunning Evidence Shows the Science Behind Speaking in Tongues" by Jessilyn Justice it said, *"Science now backs this lack of control over your tongue, essentially proving the Holy Spirit actively moves your speech pattern when speaking in tongues."* When people speak in tongues, it is not generated in the same part of the brain where our speech originates.

It is understandable if you are skeptical; however, we owe it to ourselves to partake of our divine inheritance. Remember, tongues are our private prayer language. We do not have to pursue it in public. We can do it in the comfort of our home—like I did.

If you need help, find a Spirit-filled and tongue-talking Believer where you fellowship to assist you. For the most part, they will be undercover if the gift is not reverenced in your church. I bet there is at least one babbling sheep hiding in the bunch.

At times, people struggle for years trying to speak in tongues. For some they are blocked by un-forgiveness and lack of repentance. I ministered to a woman about this and her tongues came out like an unleashed fire hydrant. She was happy; I was happy, and nobody was mad but the Devil.

When you speak in tongues, it's a bit like doing spiritual aerobics. Do it in your car, in the shower, while you are cleaning your house, or any time you want. It helps to do it under your breath when you are being harassed or you feel yourself getting upset or angry.

Tongues have a way of soothing the savage beast and you can do it as often as you want. Once you got it, it is yours. For some of y'all, it is probably nice to know it cannot be repossessed.

The New Testament accounts say the apostle Paul spoke in tongues more than anyone (1 Corinthians 14:18), and the disciples spoke in tongues too (Acts 2:4). Not long from now, you will be able to say the same thing. And, if you already do, then the next step is to help others find the bliss so they too can be catapulted into another spiritual dimension. Do not wait to be empowered on a level you cannot comprehend.

DISCIPLE ME NOW: Learn – Grow – Practice - Go
The Truth
Seven Holy Spirit Truths

- *However, when He, the Spirit of truth comes, He will guide you into all the truth; for He will not speak on His own authority, but whatever He hears He will speak; and He will tell you things to come (John 16:13)*
- *But God has revealed them to us through His Spirit. For the Spirit searches all things, yes the deep things of God (1 Corinthians 2:10)*
- *If you love me, keep My commandments. And I will pray the Father, and He will give you another Helper, that He may abide with you forever (John 14:15-16)*
- *But when the Helper comes, whom I will send to you from the Father, the Spirit of truth who proceeds from the Father, He will testify of Me (John 15:26)*
- *These things we also speak, not in words which man's wisdom teaches but which the Holy Spirit teaches, comparing spiritual things with spiritual (1 Corinthians 2:13)*
- *Not by might, nor by power, but by My Spirit, says the Lord of hosts (Zechariah 4:6)*
- *And do not grieve the Holy Spirit of God, by whom you were sealed for the day of redemption (Ephesians 4:30)*

Here are your do-it-yourself directions on how to receive this amazing gift in the privacy of your own home, just like I did. These simple instructions can also be used to minister this gift to someone else or in a group. Remember, there is no failure in trying. And, just like my Brother told me, "Don't stop until you have it."

Father said if two of us agree we can ask anything in His name and He would do it. He wants you to have the gift He left for you to receive, and I am going to stand with you, in the Spirit, until you get it. You are not alone.

Preparation for the Baptism of the Holy Spirit

First, God is giving you this gift because He loves you. He wants you to succeed on Earth. This gift is not about whether you are worthy to have it, because none of us are.

Second, If you ask God to forgive you nothing you ever did or said can hinder you from receiving this gift.

Third, You have to go to the throne of grace boldly (Hebrews 4:16), with clean hands, and a forgiving heart. He said we can not be forgiven if we are unwilling to forgive. If you have any bad feelings, bitterness, or offense in your heart toward anyone for any reason, you have to release it.

Note: Forgiving someone does not mean they are not guilty of what they did. It means you are no longer holding the wrong they did against them, which is exactly what Christ did for you.

Fourth, After you release someone, take a deep breath through your nose and blow out your mouth. By faith, you are letting go of the error of unrighteousness, healing the soul wounds, and forcing out spirits trying to hinder the flow of God through you.

Last, Forgive yourself. Releasing yourself is as important as you letting others off the hook. We all make mistakes. Hopefully, you can learn from your infractions, and you are open to the Holy Spirit to heal your heart from your self-inflicted wounds and word curses too.

After you do this, nothing can stop you from getting what God has been waiting to give you, since the day you were born…again.

Simple Steps for Receiving the Baptism of the Holy Spirit

Special Note: This is only available to those who have confessed Jesus Christ as their Lord and Savior. You can do this alone, at home, with someone else or as a group. This is also recommended for children who have confessed Christ as their Lord and Savior.

Step One: Pray the prayer of faith (Hebrews 11:1); no man calls on God
and He does not answer (Isaiah 58:9)

*Father, I honor you as the King of kings, and as the only true and living
God. Thank you for your son Jesus, and Jesus thank you for the precious Holy
Spirit. Holy Spirit, I honor you for who you are and what you are about to do.*

*Heavenly Father, I cannot thank you enough for making right all my
wrongs through your grace. Please forgive me Lord for holding grudges, being
bitter, living in un-forgiveness, resentment, and retaliating against those who
have hurt me. Forgive me for those I have hurt. Forgive me for wounding myself by not allowing your Word to penetrate the parts of me that were wounded.*

*In the name of Jesus, I bind every word curse that confines me, and I sever
those that I have spoken over others. Today, I need you to cleanse me from all
unrighteousness and anything that would hinder me from receiving the gift you
have for me. Father, reveal anything that I have forgotten? (Wait quietly to see
if He brings anything to your mind, and if He does, use the instructions above
to handle it, and then proceed.)*

*Now that my spiritual slate is clean and the enemy no longer has a legal
right to hinder this process, I take authority over the atmosphere around me,
and I bind whatever is not in alignment with my destiny. Your manifested presence, Holy Spirit, is welcome to come right now.*

*Baptize me in the fire of the Holy Spirit. Fill me with your glory, and with
the evidence of speaking in tongues. My heart is open and my mind is surrendered to the fullness of being spirit-filled right now, in Jesus' name. Come Holy
Spirit, come.*

Step Two: Close your eyes so you are not distracted and worship God.
Speak out loud and tell God how good He is, and how much you appreciate
what He has done for you; adore Him for who He is; love on Him with all your
might, all your strength, and everything in you; do not allow your mind to
wonder; take authority over your thoughts and direct them only to your risen
King

Step Three: Lay hands on yourself; once you saturate the atmosphere
with worship, call forth what is already inside of you—the rivers of living
water; you are only stirring up the anointing, the fire, and His glory; continue

to worship and let the hunger in your heart beckon for the Holy Spirit to take over your tongue (Important: You have to speak out loud for your heavenly language to come out)

Step Four: Repeat until you are speaking in your new Kingdom language; be like Jacob and wrestle with God until He gives it to you (Genesis 32:24); you will not be disappointed if you tarry until it comes

My experience did not involve any exaggerated manifestations. The bottom line is to allow God to fill you in whatever way He wants, and be open to earth-shattering theatrics, or the sound of the softest, sweetest, most gentle tongues you ever heard. It does not matter how He does it, just get it.

The Deception

Every Believer should know there is a perversion spirit mimicking the Holy Spirit called Kundalini. It is aggressively infiltrating unaware and naïve Christians. Kundalini is a familiar spirit (Leviticus 20:6). Have you seen it? Would you know it if you did? If you do not, after reading this you will.

This invasion is being pedaled down the corridors of our church like those hand-held fans the ushers pass out on a hot summer day. Remember, the devil does not have any new. He only perverts what already exists. False doctrine destabilizes Believers (Ephesians 4:14) and threatens the Kingdom of God. The Scripture clearly warns Jesus followers accordingly:

In the last days, the Lord is going to pour out His Spirit (Acts 2:17), so the enemy has to mimic the final move of God, with a bogus spirit. He knows a great harvest of souls is connected to this outpouring.

Wikipedia, states "Kundalini is described as lying "coiled" at the base of the spine, represented as either a goddess or sleeping serpent waiting to be awakened." Sir John Woodroofe coined the phrase "serpent power" to identify Kundalini. Kundalini is a spirit impersonating the Holy Spirit. Arousing Kundalini is said to be for the purpose of spiritual enlightenment and Kundalini awakening results in deep meditation, enlightenment, and bliss.[19]

When the Kundalini is awakened, here are some of the physical and psychological problems associated, and how the manifestations are exhibited. Maybe you or someone you know exhibits these signs. If you are not seeing it already, this will be good preparation for, not if, but when you do.

Wikipedia contributors described Kundalini manifestations as follows:[20]

- Involuntary jerks, tremors, shaking, itching, tingling, and crawling sensations, especially in the arms and legs
- Energy rushes or feelings of electricity circulating the body
- Intense heat (sweating) or cold, especially as energy is experienced passing through the chakras
- Diminished or conversely extreme sexual desire sometimes leading to a state of constant or whole-body orgasm
- Emotional numbness
- Antisocial tendencies
- Mood swings with periods of depression or mania
- Pains in different areas of the body, especially back and neck
- Trance-like and altered states of consciousness
- Disrupted sleep pattern (periods of insomnia or oversleeping)
- Bliss, feelings of infinite love and universal connectivity, transcendent awareness

When we see these so-called manifestations, what we are really seeing is a perversion of the Spirit of God. God does everything decent and in order, and anything causing us to lose control is not of God.

The Holy Spirit does not resemble a snake, or body convulsions that mimic someone having a seizure, or rhythmic motions that look like someone having intercourse in public. He will not cause you to roll around on the floor on top of people of the opposite sex, in His honor.

If you or someone you know is infected with Kundalini, follow these guidelines to get rid of it:

- Confess to God what you did that connected you with Kundalini; if you do not know ask God to reveal it or seek someone with a Word of Knowledge gift to assist you
- Repent for opening the door and being in agreement with a demonic representative of the Holy Spirit
- Turn away from what you were or are doing immediately
- Ask the Holy Spirit to cleanse you of that spirit and then bind it
- Command Kundalini to leave your body quickly

- Take authority over any manifestations (i.e. pain in lower extremities or lower back, rebellion or any resistance to the spirit leaving in the name of Jesus)
- Declare you are the temple of the living God and command everything to bow its knee to Jesus Christ; then command that it must go
- Speak relevant Scriptures over yourself as the demonic spirit is exiting until it is gone
- By faith, close all the doors that were opened by this spirit
- Cover yourself in the blood of Jesus after you put on the armor of God in Ephesians 6

Now, be prepared for people who may reject what you are saying. It is difficult to admit you have been entertaining a phony spirit. This revelation can seriously derail an already defective spiritual encounter. Pray and ask God for wisdom on how and if you are to proceed in revealing the truth.

God is a jealous God (Deuteronomy 6:15), but not in an envious or selfish way like us. Anything that distracts us from the real thing is stealing the worship and relationship that only belongs to Him. He has no tolerance for the adoration *He deserves* to be given to anyone else. Hence, He made it a commandment to have no other god before Him (Exodus 20:3). He will also not compete for your loyalty or affection. Why? Because, He does not have to.

Every living and breathing creature exists by the grace of His love. The trees lift their branches, the sea stops at the shore, and the sun stays in its cycle because He said so. The moon rises in succession with the stars—in honor and submission to God's words. His will is for us not to give His worship to another.

God said, *When the enemy comes in like a flood, The Spirit of the Lord will lift up a standard against him (Isaiah 59:19).* Finally, never forget the enemy wants to compromise your effectiveness by infecting you with a knockoff, if he can. Who doesn't know there is nothing like the real thing? If he gets you spewing his knockoff, then next he wants you to multiply so you are peddling his erroneous delusion fast and hard, down the throats, and into the hearts of your fellow brothers and sisters in Christ. Hopefully, now you know the difference.

In closing, if you are being pushed or knocked down by someone laying hands on you, be concerned. Falling down does not mean the Spirit is moving.

The Holy Spirit does not have to put you on the floor to do His business, but it does not mean He will not. Now, should you end up down there supernaturally, not because everyone else is doing it, praise God! We do Christendom a huge disservice when we fake being slain in the Spirit.

THE PLAYERS: GOD

The Creator

THE TRUTH: There is only one true living God and everlasting King (Jeremiah 10:10)

THE DECEPTION: There is no God. *The fool has said in his heart, "There is no God" (Psalm 14:1)*

How exactly do you describe the one who is the source of life for all living things? Even His name is sacred, which is why one of the Ten Commandments says don't use it in vain (Exodus 20:7). Outlined here are three things to know if we want to outsmart the enemy and ascend into our destinies. We have to believe God exists, worship Him in Spirit and truth, and obey everything He says to do. The absence of any one of these, and we are on a slippery slope to becoming spiritual road kill.

Before I begin this discourse, I invite you to ponder this vitally important question: do you love God? Four little words can change the landscape of your entire life. Most people, on some level, know God loves them. The question I'm posing to you today is, Do *you* love Him? You should be able to answer that question in scriptural confidence. Most Believers think they love God, but they do not, and this is why.

Obedience Is Love

God is love (1 John 4:8), and He wants us to love Him because He loves us. There is nothing worse than loving someone—and that love is not reciprocated. He demonstrated His love toward us through the action of sacrificing

His son, Jesus, and we express our love toward Him through our obedience (John 14:15).

Obedience is God's love language. Do you speak it, or are you a foreigner in His Kingdom? Let me ask the question again, "Do you love God?" The only way you can answer *yes* is if you keep His Word. Obedience is not a feeling; it is a decision to do what He says.

When we do not obey God, we give the enemy a legal right, in the spirit, to assault us. He enjoys the access it gives him. He knows God is just, and He cannot go against His own word, although He might desperately want to on our behalf.

Obedience is also an act of submission. We submit our will to the will of God—not to do whatever we want or feel like doing. I am one-hundred percent sure Jesus wanted not to die if it were possible, which is why He said, "Can this cup pass from me"? (Matthew 26:39). Your obedience is nothing short of what Jesus had to do on the cross. He was obedient until death. In order for us to be obedient, something has to die and often more than once.

The main road to the character of Christ is obeying Him in all things. Each time we choose it, we go from glory to glory, which is a path of divine ascension. The process requires us to take every thought captive. All of our feelings, thoughts, and emotions have to line up with the Word of God to be able to do this. Once we recognize we are in disobedience, we can choose to love God by correcting our behavior.

Each one of us has to make *obeying* our number-one priority. In our relationship with God there is nothing more important. Once we get this, we can teach it to our children, and integrate it into our church services, discipleship classes, and Christian conferences. All of us should endeavor to practice, encourage, acknowledge, and reward it. If we individually do our part, then collectively we will all benefit.

Liars Beware

1 John 2:4 says:"*He who says, "I know Him," and does not keep His commandments, is a liar, and the truth is not in him.*" If we ever wondered if we know God, this Scripture gives us a simple way to find out. No one has to speculate on where they stand.

When I was growing up, my mother said there are two things people do not like: one is a thief, and the other is a liar—because both cannot be trusted.

She usually made that declaration in the face of one of my siblings not coming clean about something, and Neicey had the art of lying perfected. I think baby girl came here with a spirit of not telling the truth when she was a kid. Thank God she grew out of it.

Right here, right now, we can make the decision, by faith, to be obedient. If we do, this can be the match to ignite revival in our hearts. All God wants is for us to love Him and He tells us how to do it. In essence, it means surrender trying to do it our way, and yield to doing it His, because then He knows we love Him.

God

Christians believe God exists. If you do not, nothing I write after this will matter. You have to get this part right. We can experience God, but no one has ever seen Him (John 1:18). It is by faith we must believe He is, and He rewards those who diligently seek Him (Hebrews 11:6).

Scripture tells us every created human being knows that God exists. Anyone who says otherwise, including atheist and agnostics, is admitting they are in agreement with deception. You may not like what I am saying, nevertheless it is truth.

For since the creation of the world His invisible attributes are clearly seen, being understood by the things that are made, even His eternal power and Godhead, so that they are without excuse (Romans 1:20)

Believe

For those who want proof God is real, just ask Him. Once He reveals Himself, we will never wonder again. Like Jesus told Thomas, His Disciple: blessed are those who do not see and believe (John 20:29).

It is interesting that the Bible says the demons believe and tremble (James 2:19). We say we believe, but we are unmoved by the things we are doing that God disapproves of. The fear of God is the beginning of knowledge. Not fear as in being dreadful, but as in reverence (Proverbs 1:7).

The Greek verb for *believe* is *pisteuo*, which means *to entrust, have faith in, be persuaded by action* or *have active confidence in*. God insists on *pisteuo*, which is the gateway to His heart for all who are aligned with Him in Spirit.

Some things can be better understood when we experience them, like God and eating ice cream.

Worship

We were created to worship God. If you have a problem doing what you were created to do, find the obstruction, because *"God is a Spirit, and those who worship Him must worship Him in spirit and in truth (John 4:24)."* There is no way around worshipping.

One of the most powerful moments I experienced with God was not in church. It was as I worshipped in the privacy of my home. It happened as I prayed the names of God. I had a list on my wall that I referred to often, and one day I just began to pray God's nature based on that list.

My adoration went something like this. The first name on the list was *Jehovah Tsidkenu*, the Lord our righteousness. I wanted right standing to prevail in my life. *Jehovah Jireh*, the Lord who provides, was next. Everybody calls on Him. Can I get a witness? More of us need to call on *Jehovah Rapha*, the Lord who heals. He has the best healthcare plan in the world, and it's free. He paid the price so we do not have to. Our only co-pay is to believe. *Jehovah Shalom*, the Lord is peace, and *El-Elyon*, the Most High God were on the list too. In total, there were twelve names I prayed.

Every time I engaged God by His name it seemed He stood up at His throne and rushed right to where I was. His response was so affectionate. It felt like a fully engulfed fire. The reverence we are giving Him is like pouring gasoline on a burning inferno. The more we tell Him about Himself, the more He releases His glory, His love, the essence of His Spirit … and it goes on. It is so amazing I almost do not know how to describe it. I invite you to try it for yourself.

God is looking for the reflection of Himself in you. When he hears His name being lifted up, we have become a channel to reflect His nature, and it draws Him to us. When He comes, we can literally feel the atmosphere shift. As I worshipped, I was consumed in His Shekinah glory, and Heaven came to kiss the earth, where I was kneeling.

Behind the Veil

Initially, my time of prayer and worship happened mostly when I was driving my car. On occasion, the shower was a nice place to talk to God. There were moments when I prayed sitting on my bed when I woke up, or at night before I went to sleep. Those instances worked rather well for me, that is, until the day God impressed on my Spirit, my not bowing down before Him was an issue of pride.

I did not realize it was difficult for me to get on my knees until He brought it to my attention. The places I prayed were not the problem, it was the condition of my heart God wanted to address. He has a way of rattling my cage, from time to time, and it usually leaves me completely laid out on the floor. He will get us down there one way or another.

The more God pruned my heart of stone and turned it into flesh, there was a direct connection to my knees bending. As I learned to obey Him, He drew me nearer, which is not possible unless we let something go. It became easy to lower myself in His presence.

Since then, not only have I learned to bow down before Him, but there have been times, in the privacy of my own home, when the Father beckoned me in my birthday suit. That means He draws us before His throne in the state of His original design, naked.

Before the Fall of mankind, it was natural to walk around in only our skin talking to God. There was nothing strange about it. Covering up was the first gesture of shame and being unclean after Adam and Eve disobeyed God in the Garden (Genesis 3:7). Their eyes were opened to being naked and they hid from God. When we come to His throne, and there is not a stitch of fabric between us and Him, something so natural and so profound transpires. It seems we can even hear better.

We must reopen the altars in our churches as well as in our hearts. Dust off the place where we bend our knees in the sanctuary, and lower ourselves in humility. Where worship is optional, revival is not possible. Our knees are too tender. The condition of the church, our families, and the world should dictate our knees be raw from constant use.

Have you ever seen the whole congregation go to the altar, bow down and cry out to God in repentance, for supernatural intervention, or to be consumed with His Spirit? Does your church even have an altar? If you have children, have you ever bowed before God and invited your children to join you? If not, this is a perfect time to start.

Where are the hearts willing to pull on the hem of His Spirit? Is there nothing in our lives that warrants this level of desperation?

If we are in a relationship with the God of Abraham, Isaac, and Jacob, inevitably something will have us bombard the altar and fall prostrate on our faces until He answers. Are the days of travail gone? Not so, says His Servant, not so.

Each time I was interrupted as I worshipped—it was because the person who wanted me to quiet down, or quit, was uncomfortable with how I worshipped. When we worship God loudly, it does not make us bad. If we are quiet, it does not make us good. I would not go around interrupting people who are quiet saying, "Can't you be a little louder, God can't hear you."

We are all different, and God made us that way for a reason. We have to embrace and honor the differences in how we worship. I am mentioning this because you are going to need it should you be privileged to be where revival hits. Get ready. You might want to lose your religious guardrails.

Worship is not complicated. It is adoration. When we worship, we are simply telling God how off-the-chain and absolutely amazing He is. Who does not like to be adored? God loves it so much, He went as far as to say, *"Let everything that has breath praise the Lord (Psalm 150:6)."*

Any questions now about who should be praising Him? He said, "Everything with breath," and for me, that included our four-pound with-an-attitude Chihuahua, Prince Jonas, and his younger brother, a sweet Border Terrier named King James.

When was the last time you did nothing but tell God how amazing He is or, how much you adore Him? He wants to hear us whisper sweet nothings in His ear. No matter who we are, at some point or another, God is going to get the worship He deserves. Eventually, every knee will bow and every tongue will confess (Romans 14:11).

In preparation for revival we can all raise the bar on our worship. When it starts—and the people come in off the street, falling at the altar, screaming to God how they might be saved—would we know what to do? Or, would we try to keep everything neat and tidy as not to mess up the religious flow we're conditioned by? Heads-up, it is not going to work.

Every Knee Shall Bow

Worship encounters, like the one I mentioned, were possible because the Holy Spirit taught me the importance of humbling myself before God. It was a great awakening, the day I was informed my knees had another purpose other than using them to look under the bed for my shoes. At some point, we have to bow in a gesture of reverence to a God who is Holy, just, righteous, strong and mighty, sovereign, merciful, and gracious.

As my relationship with God grew stronger, He began to require a more intimate and mature interaction between us. Much like we do with children. We expect two-year-olds to have poopy diapers and temper tantrums, but when they are ten, that behavior would not be tolerated. God is the same way about worship. He wants us to mature in this area as well.

Spirit

God is a spirit; it means he is not flesh and bones. But, His presence is as real as if He were. Spirit-filled Believers have experienced or encountered the Spirit of God, right? You have, haven't you? If you have not, you are due for a God encounter. Do not let any grass grow under your feet until you do. I encourage you to keep pulling on Him until you have an undeniable experience with the King.

DISCIPLE ME NOW: Learn – Grow – Practice – Go
The Truth
God Is

- *I am the Alpha and the Omega, the Beginning and the End, says the Lord, who is and who was and who is to come, the Almighty (Revelation 1:8)*
- *Behold, I am the Lord, the God of all flesh. Is there anything too hard for Me (Jeremiah 32:27)*
- *I am the Lord, who makes all things, Who stretches out the heavens all alone, Who spreads abroad the earth by Myself (Isaiah 44:24)*

His Character
- God is holy and He wants you to be holy, in your conduct too (1 Peter 1:15)
- God is good (Mark 10:18)

- God is righteous (Psalm11:7)
- God can do the impossible (Luke 18:27)
- God is omnipotent (all powerful)
- God is unchanging (Hebrews 13:8)
- God is sovereign (2 Samuel 7:22)
- God is wise (1 Timothy 1:17)
- God is faithful (Psalm 89:1-2)

Where Is God

- He is everywhere and nothing is hidden from Him (Psalm 139:7-12)
- *The eyes of the Lord are in every place, keeping watch on the evil and the good (Proverbs 15:3)*

What Has He Done

- *For God so loved the world that He gave His only begotten Son, that whoever believes in Him should not perish but have everlasting life (John 3:16)*
- *For behold, He who forms the mountains, and creates the wind, who declares to man what his thought is, and who makes the morning darkness, who treads the high places of the earth— the Lord God of hosts is His name (Amos 4:13)*
- *But the Lord shall endure forever; He has prepared His throne for judgment. He shall judge the world in righteousness, and He shall administer judgment for the peoples in uprightness (Psalm 9:7-8)*

The Deception

Listed below are a few common lies being said about God.

- God is unfair—FALSE (Deuteronomy 32:4)
- There is more than one God, with a capital *G*—FALSE (Jeremiah 10:10)
- God lies—FALSE (Numbers 23:19)
- God is mad at us—FALSE (Jeremiah 29:11)
- God will share His worship—FALSE (Exodus 34:4)
- God is jealous, like us—FALSE
- God wants to punish us—FALSE
- God is too holy for us to talk to Him—FALSE
- God is not interested in what is going on in our lives—FALSE

"When purpose is not known, abuse is inevitable."

Myles Munroe

Section IV

The Plan
Know God's Plan for Victory

THE PLAN

The ultimate plan of God is an invitation for all Christians to become disciples. It is the single most important thing we can do to succeed in His Kingdom, and below are three components we can prepare to embrace in the process.

First, know you will experience a period of transition. We have to come from being out of alignment with God to walking in right order with Him, and that takes time.

Second, understand that discipleship is the core of the Great Commission, which I will discuss in detail. It is never too late to get this badge of honor no matter how long you have been perched on that pew.

Lastly, we all have to be equipped to engage in spiritual warfare. If offers more ways for us to have victory than any other area. If we continue to ignore and abandon this strategy, our demise is inevitable. Outside the neglect of making disciples, teaching Believers how to fight is another reason why we fail.

The Wake-Up Call

The door of God's plan is often opened when life brings us to the end of ourselves and there is no one and nowhere else to turn. That happened to me the day my mother died. My whole world collapsed and continued to tumble for the next three years.

Looking back on that dreadful day, I can see it was when God's plan started to take shape in my life. Failure, pain, tragedy, and disappointment are always a good place to scope the landscape to see if God is drawing us near. He frequently uses discomfort as an invitation into His embrace.

This is what happened. The phone rang in my office and my cousin said, "Vivian get to the hospital," and slammed the phone down. She knew I am an extreme extrovert and highly animated. Corralling my unbridled passion could be a nightmare, and she could not control it over the phone…hence, she dropped the bomb and hung up.

My heart raced and the adrenaline in my veins strangled my breathing. Inside I had an inclination whatever was going on was bad, and somehow I knew it was my mom.

As I rushed to the hospital, I wrestled with God as I negotiated for her life. My mind seesawed with the possibilities of what happened. I saw myself jumping on the hospital bed and shaking her until she opened her eyes.

Back then, I was the average Sunday-go-to-church, pew-warming, don't-have-a-clue Christian. My church attendance was regular enough for me to not think I was not a complete heathen.

Sadly, the love of my life was gone when I arrived. Mom's sudden passing was the wake-up call that went unanswered, for years. Destiny was trying to get in, but I had the door locked and bolted.

After I woke up from the trauma of sudden-death syndrome, I remember feeling as if I was kicked off my mom's spiritual coattail. Not knowing who was going to take her place tormented my soul. Her prayers gave me confidence, but it did nothing to help me establish my own relationship with Jesus.

She was everything to me God should have been, and after she died—I did not have a choice, but to seek God for myself. Unfortunately, I wandered in the wilderness, almost as long as the Israelites did, before that thought moved from my head to my heart.

Losing her led me to the love affair of my life, but it was not with her. I loved my mother from the top of my head to the tips of my toes. But, even though Mom was dead, my connection with her continued as if she never left.

When I was sad, I talked to her. When I got a new man or my relationships went south, she got all the juicy details. We celebrated my new job opportunities. I burdened her with every aspect of my life while she lay waiting in paradise.

The day the Holy Spirit told me, "Your mother is your idol," I was undone. It felt like someone snatched the air from my lungs. God will give us the truth about ourselves in a way that is indisputable. Guilty as charged. I had given my mother, not God, lordship in my life.

My mom was short in stature, but tall in strength, and her sweet continence touched many lives. The pedigree of her personality was love for her family and people in general. She would always say, "Vivian, you can sell ice to the Eskimos, and do anything you set your mind to as long as you are willing to work.' I believed her. It seemed I could accomplish anything as long as she was by my side. Life was grand until my false sense of security—I wore like an undergarment—was stripped away.

The Yellow Brick Road to providence I was on was only in my imagination. Instead, I was walking a labyrinth of deception paved with vain philosophies, worldly wisdom, and self-will. This fiasco was propelled by misguided faith, which took me into debt and farther away from my spiritual inheritance.

Kryptonite is to Superman what carnal advice is to a Christian—and I got my share of it from the self-help gurus I frequented. My soul-ish pursuits disguised as destiny afforded me moderate success, but accomplishment is not an indication of God's favor and neither does failure mean God's disdain.

For He makes His sun rise on the evil and on the good, and sends rain on the just and on the unjust (Matthew 5:45)

Parents want the best for their children, and God the Father is no different (Matthew 7:11).

Years after becoming a disciple, I discovered my mother's desires for me, and her love, although extraordinary, did not compare to God's. He outdid her in every category. Anything anyone does, did or did not do, with us, for us or against us, does not matter because God's plan is sufficient all by itself.

God is sovereign. All He wants is for us to voluntarily bring ourselves to His throne so He can guide every aspect of our lives. If someone had discipled me when I got baptized at twelve I may not have spent decades wandering in the wilderness of carnality.

The Sheep That Swim

In order to make the shift and overthrow the plot of the enemy, we have to graduate from **PEWniversity**, which means sitting idly in the pews. If we do not, our destinies could die right there on that bench.

We must uproot every pew potato and declare; "Tuition denied!" Are you willing to exchange religious pageantry for spiritual maturity? If you have been in church for any length of time, chances are you have already been socialized to be counter productive to growing in practice and relationship.

Great numbers of people are going to be unwilling to separate from the crowd. You do not have to be one of them.

For wide is the gate and broad is the way that leads to destruction, and there are many who go in by it (Matthew 7:13)

Of course, change is uncomfortable, messy, and sometimes frightening, but nonetheless it is necessary. We cannot remain as we are—as the most powerful people on the planet, the cost of doing so cannot be calculated in this realm.

Here is what we need to do. We have to metaphorically turn around. We are not leaving our churches, but we are shifting our paradigms—and swimming upstream. We need to do what salmon do. Their lifestyle provides the perfect analogy. Salmon are distinguished from other fish because they swim upstream. They go *against* the current. It is in their genetic profile to swim head-on into strong waters, which is exactly the strategy we have to embrace.

About eighty percent of the church is going in the opposite direction of the Great Commission, which is to make disciples. It will take a made-up mind, along with courage and supernatural help to see us through. If a salmon stays where they are born, they die, and they cannot multiply. The same is true for us. If we do not fly off that pew, our true destinies might never see the light of day. There are people waiting to be impacted by what God created YOU to do.

For many are called, but few are chosen (Matthew 22:14)

Why is it folk get saved and then all of a sudden they are sensitive and temperamental? But when they were in the world, they were in bar brawls, people talked about them like a dog, cussed them out, and some got beat to a pulp—and they didn't faint. Often, they came back swinging. Now they are saved and the spiritual defibrillator is working overtime.

I watch so many Christians get their panties in a bunch over the smallest of offenses. Trust me, I use to do it too. Makes one feel like we are fighting side-by-side with a bunch of malnourished, spiritually retarded, and unequipped people saying they are born-again. Sometimes, I want to ask the question, "Born-again of what?" We cannot be in spiritual combat with soldiers who are sensitive, fragile, easily offended, and unequipped.

People are on the battlefield, and they have never gone through boot camp. And if that isn't bad enough, then they get promoted to leadership with no training, no equipment, and no clue of what is really happening. Then the casualties of friendly fire start stacking up and the wounded begin marching out the door. We can get mad about what I am saying—or we can get equipped.

Are you in the combat zone without your spiritual gear mentioned in Ephesians 6:11-18? We can be victorious over the enemy who is trying to steal our destiny with the right tools.

Now, beware; some of the opposition you might encounter will come from within the walls of the church. It will be your fellow brothers and sisters in Christ, or the ones pretending they are. They will be your treasures of torment and create plenty of opportunities for you to practice.

In our natural families we have disagreements, conflict, and children who do not know how to act. It is no different in the family of God. When people get saved they begin the process of changing, and we have to be patient with them as they do.

Work through it, have some patience, and give grace. Keep in mind: Jesus went through the same thing with the religious folk of His day, and we are to follow in His steps (1 Peter 2:21), and while we are at it, we might as well taste in His sufferings (Philippians 3:10). If you are doing this like Jesus did, eventually you too will ask "Can this cup pass from me" (Matthew 26:39).

The Great Commission

Jesus knew if we became His disciples, it would be a game changer. It would automatically separate us from the crowd. It is the easiest way to learn how to come from amongst them, and is a sure path to victory.

Come out from among them and be separate, says the Lord
(2 Corinthians 6:16)

Becoming and making disciples is a biblical mandate uttered from the lips of God. It is expressed in one of the most visible, but equally disregarded, Scriptures in the Bible.

The Key to Destiny

Go therefore and make disciples of all nations, baptizing them in the name of the Father and of the Son and of the Holy Spirit, teaching them to observe all things that I have commanded you (Matthew 28:19-20)

Are you familiar with this Scripture? This is "The Great Commission." We cannot afford to neglect, minimize, or ignore what holds the key to real VS perceived success in the Kingdom of God. If we embrace this verse, we will have a considerable advantage over the 1.7 billion Christians who are not discipled. Now, that would make us a serious threat to the Kingdom of Darkness. We will talk more about that later.

Discipleship is not optional. There is no Plan *B*, and pew-sitting doesn't even put us in the game. Being discipled is an act of submission and obedience to the Word of God, not man. God is not impressed with works. He is awed and undone by our obedience to Him.

Jesus demonstrated the Great Commission when He left the Synagogue and interacted with the people who needed what He had. Once they accepted His offer of salvation, He immediately began to teach them what He knew. He did not need to raise money to disciple people, convene a board meeting, or design a marketing plan. There is no time for making excuses. If you are born-again, that is your permit to become a disciple and make them too.

Did you ever notice in Scripture when the disciples accepted the invitation to a new life they did not continue doing what they were doing when Jesus found them? There was a drastic change in direction. Read for yourself the two most talked about conversions in Scripture.

- Matthew's – Matthew 9:9-13
- Saul's – Acts 9:1-31

Once the disciples were equipped—not perfect, but prepared—Jesus commissioned them to go do exactly what He did. If all the people who sit in the pews on Sunday mornings were equipped and released into the highways and the byways to do what Jesus did, it would tilt the earth.

The Numbers Don't Lie

Several months ago, I read an insightful article about a non-denominational, multi-generational, Evangelical, Christian, mega church that thought they were making disciples. Willow Creek Community (WCC) located in a Chicago suburb is not just any church. It is recognized as "the" leader of how we should run our churches.

WCC spent millions doing church and then telling others how to do it. They were so confident about what they were doing they commissioned a million-dollar qualitative, multi-year, multi-campus study to validate their convictions. The survey measured the effectiveness of the pastor's philosophical and ministerial approach to running churches.

Sadly, the findings were the complete opposite of what they expected, and they were shocked. The Pastor of WCC, Pastor Bill Hybel, was convinced they were making disciples. The study revealed, in fact, they were not.

All the religious rhetoric, pageantry, and programs they created were not doing the job. In his own words the Pastor said, "We made a mistake," and boy was it a big one. All that money spent to find out what so many Believers already know.

Many of us have been victims of religious charades served to us in the name of Jesus. Our time has been wasted and our emotions taxed. The rapidly declining attendance is in direct correlation to this dilemma.

Even though Pastor Hybel missed the mark, he did Christianity a favor by failing. Some of us have waited a long time to get the proof that much of what the church is doing to make followers is not working. But, he didn't faint because he made a mistake. He took the information and revamped his approached. Nowhere in Scriptures does it say making mistakes is prohibited.

The Barna Group conducted a comprehensive, multi-phase research study in December 2015 that revealed "Christian adults believe their churches are doing well when it comes to discipleship: 52 percent of those who have attended church in the past six months say their church "definitely does a good job helping people grow spiritually" and another 40 percent say it "probably" does so. Additionally, two-thirds of Christians who have attended church in the past six months and consider spiritual growth important say their church places "a lot" of emphasis on spiritual growth (67%); another 27 percent say their church gives "some" emphasis. Church leaders, conversely, tend to believe the opposite is true."[21]

When the process of being discipled—based on relevant activities—was assessed, only twenty percent of Christians were participating. "Yet, the research reveals little correlation between activity and perceived growth, further revealing the disconnect between how people think about their spirituality and what's actually happening in their lives"[22] We call that deception.

Those startling statistics are compounded by the US Census Bureau reporting over 4,000 churches close annually, and only 1,000 started. Every year almost 2.7 million Christians fall into inactivity.[23] Why is that, when over four billion people need to be evangelized?

Also, according to the US Census Bureau records we need at least 38,000 churches—right now—to keep up with the population growth. There is no time to waste when souls hang in the balance. Frankly, we must plead and pray for every church leader throughout the world, housing the laborers, to equip and release them pronto.

There are thousands of willing vessels decaying on the pews, who are ready to do the work of the ministry. We should do an alter call for those ready and see how many people come up. We might be surprised. There is a reward for our obedience on this side of Heaven, and an even greater one waiting inside the pearly gates.[24]

One of my motivations behind writing this book came from my own experience as a Believer, healing and deliverance minister, Sunday School teacher, and missionary. About ninety-seven percent of the people I interact with, in each of these arenas, who are Christian, have not been discipled or equipped in any formal way. There is a serious drought in the making of disciples and it is taking a toll on Christendom.

This deficit is a direct assault on God's plan. Believers are being targeted and distracted from being discipled—because the enemy knows this is the primary pillar needed to build the Kingdom of God on earth and in the hearts of man. Here are some benefits to being discipled.

At the end of the day, most people want and need three things (in this order):

- How to help ourselves
- How to help our families
- How to help and impact the world around us

Call it the Church's Maslow Hierarchy of Needs. The Great Commission works if you work it and it lines us up with all three.

There is a lot to grasp about becoming a disciple, and we are not going to learn it all overnight. Make it a personal mission, to be a dynamic disciple of Jesus Christ. For many years, I lived with the motivation, that at the end of the day, Jesus would say, *"Well done thy good and faithful servant"* (Matthew 25:21). This mindset helped me to shift my behavior on a daily basis to accommodate the life of Christ working in and through me.

The process of imitating the Savior and maturing in His statues is a life-long course of study. For your reference, may some of the benefits to being disciples and the things that stirred me to righteousness help you do the same. Ponder this list:

- Get the revelation of His love for yourself and then you can share it with others
- Practice the art of dying to self
- Experience deliverance and learn self-deliverance
- Read the Bible on a regular basis, actually daily would be good, and read out loud as often as possible (Romans 10:17)
- Get tools to help you study the Bible and most bible study apps include the tools we need including *Strong's Concordance*, *Matthew Henry's Commentary* and different versions of the Bible (2 Timothy 2:15)
- Find someone to hold you accountable for maturing in your walk
- Be teachable and maintain a position of learning even when you think you know
- Make sure you are on the right path—Jesus Christ is the only way (John 14:16)
- Anticipate doing greater than Jesus did (John 14:12)
- Focus on developing the character of Christ as outline in the fruit of the Spirit and strive to display His nature always (Galatians 5:22-23)
- Resist exercising and/or exhibiting the works of the flesh (Galatians 5:19-21)
- Accept you will make mistakes and do things wrong
- Be quick to repent and forgive

Getting saved is important, but growing is critical. God is not looking for religious vegans, He wants spiritual carnivores. At some point, we have to get off the milk and start chewing on some meat.

For everyone who partakes only of milk is unskilled in the word of righteousness, for he is a babe. But solid food belongs to those who are of full age, that is, those who by reason of use have their senses exercised to discern both good and evil (Hebrews 5:13-14)

A dear friend, Soldier on the battle field and colleague, Apostle Doctor Judy Bauer, has an amazing discipleship training program called KAM, which is now in over forty countries. As a graduate of KAM's Directors Evangelism and Discipleship Administrators Training, I learned ten basic Bible studies. They are a great starting point for every Believer:

- Salvation
- Baptism in the Holy Spirit
- Power of the Tongue
- Water Baptism/Child Dedication
- Prayer and Faith
- Principals of Giving
- Healing
- Church/Body of Christ
- Praise and Worship
- Communion

We cannot go wrong with these. Keep in mind, un-discipled Believers are easily offended, typically ineffective, or generally not active in ministry. This makes them unlikely to reach their full spiritual potential or fulfill their divine destiny.

Disciples are not swayed by every wind and doctrine, and being discipled is an asset. Plus it's like getting a double shot of espresso injected directly into our spiritual immune system. Then, when the wolves in sheep's clothing come, and they are coming, we will not be their victim or their host.

You might be living a great life, but that does not mean you are living your God life. Your best life is within the parameters of His plan as a disciple. Anything outside of that is your will, not His.

The Battle Begins

A few years ago I led a para-ministry in Oceanside. The goal was to provide activities that support the church, but we were not a church. We brought restoration and healing to spiritually wounded and estranged Believers so they could return to the fold.

The Lord said, "I want you to teach My people how to fight, as well as how to language My Kingdom properly." His mandate has taken on a life of its own. He also said, "Hurting Christians cannot be effective in the work of the ministry until they themselves are healed and delivered."

It is ironic my path brings me to spiritual combat training considering some forty years ago I was being tormented by a bully, because I was afraid to fight back. Boy, have things changed. Not only have I learned how to do battle in the spirit, but I had the pleasure of meeting the greatest fighter of all time, the late Muhammad Ali. Now how cool is that?

My training ground for learning to fight was on the inner city streets of Milwaukee, Wisconsin. When I was in junior high, a girl in my neighborhood—who was a bully—forced me into the ring. She threatened to beat me up on the way to school, during school, and on the way home. To this day, I don't know why.

I did everything I could to avoid crossing her path. She caused me to carry a backpack of fear. The thought of that girl gave me high blood pressure. What made it so bad was she lived next door to my best friend.

It was impossible to avoid her stalking. I'd get trapped in my best friend's house because she'd threatened to beat me up when I came out. The only way I could avoid a thrashing from her was to call my mother and have her come get me. Well, that did not last long.

My short, bow-legged mama would put her pistol in her jacket and come get me. It was a good feeling to make it home without being beat down. Unbeknownst to me, my mama had had enough. "That's it," she said. "I'm not coming over there to get you anymore. Either you kick her behind, or I'm going to kick yours." As if one threat of getting my butt beat wasn't enough, I had to choose which one I feared the most. Easy answer: my mother. I had to live with her.

Mom suspected something had to give. She knew if I did not learn to take up for myself, living in the inner city, I would not survive. One way or another,

I had to figure out how to protect myself, and that meant facing my greatest fear: the bully.

In our neighborhood, on Twentieth Street and Cherry, standing up to a bully was a rite of passage. Today fighting could cost your child their life. The next time I was threatened, I mustered up the courage to strike first with hopes that I'd get the upper hand. Her threats were like clockwork, so it was just a matter of time before she taunted me again.

When she came after me that last time, all I remember was jumping off the stairs on top of her. I was swinging my fist as fast as I could, hoping they would land somewhere near her nose. When we were finally pulled apart, I was not sure who won. But, I can tell you this, she never came after me again.

If we do not learn how to fight in the spirit, we will continue to get harassed, beat up, and spiritually assaulted. Furthermore, we cannot fight a spiritual battle with natural tools. Spiritual warfare training has to be foundational for all Believers.

Darkness Does Not Discriminate

My first scuffle with the dark side was pretty scary. Mind you, I was not an actively practicing Christian at the time. What I know now is we must learn how to walk in our spiritual authority, weather the attacks of the enemy, and push back the Kingdom of Darkness. If we don't, we will become victims— and eventually casualties—of war. We have to fight. Warfare is not optional, it is inevitable.

The day Mom died, something very strange happened. We cannot comprehend spiritual things through carnal lenses. I was too busy dining at the world's buffet and dancing with death to be of any real effect. I was blind then, but now I see. Demonic activity was happening right in front of me and I was clueless. Isaiah said it best:

They do not know or understand; For He has shut their eyes, so that they cannot see;And their hearts, so that they cannot understand (Isaiah 44:18)

We were in the emergency room of St. Joseph's hospital mourning Mom's passing. She died of natural causes driving down the street in her car. Her body was still warm, as I held her hand in a room filled with people crying. I was on her right side, at the head of the bed, and her ex was on the left across from me. Family and friends surrounded her, separating the two of us.

In the midst of us, grieving, he blurted out, "Can I clip some of her hair?" I instantly sobered up. Yes, I know sometimes people want a keepsake of the loved one they are going to miss, however, in this case I could feel something very uneasy. Sternly I said, "No!" not giving what he said another thought.

Then he said, "Can I clip some of her toe nails?" If drowning in a sea of emotions was not enough, now I was being re-traumatized by this man wanting a token from my dead mother. Why did he want a piece of her? I do not watch scary movies, and all of a sudden I was starring in one. Not on my watch, and my response again was "No!"

Clearly, he was going to persist. If you ever see a black woman blushing, make sure it is not a volcano about to erupt. One more question like that, and I thought I might have to serve up an inner-city beat down.

We looked each other in the eye and I noticed his pupils covered his entire eyeball. He had no white space. Was I tripping? Then the lights went dim and everyone around Mom's bed was sucked to the wall, except him and me. This was not a dream.

Our eyes locked in an intense dialogue with no exchange of words. Everything in me said I was face-to-face with the devil or somebody in his immediate family. Time stopped while we wrestled in the spirit and it felt like an eternity.

With much effort, I untangled myself from our gaze and screamed, "Get out!" Instantly, the lights flickered back to normal, and everyone was sucked back to the bed. He abruptly turned around, left, and we never saw him again. I was completely freaked out, but I mainted my cool.

Nobody seemed aware of what just happened, and I was so spiritually inept I did not say a word. What exactly would I have said anyway? I did not know I was engaged in warfare, and I attempted to use my natural courage to thwart a spiritual attack. It does not work. We cannot counter the darts of the enemy being spiritually slothful, mediocre, or religiously perverse. Looking back, I know grace saved my behind, for sure.

Get with the Program

The process of being transformed from a Church Goer and Pew Warmer to a disciple is the most rewarding thing we will ever do. The religious paradigm of how we do church can desensitize a Believer and encourage complacency. Millions are invited to the pew, but few are courted to come off it.

Saints want the benefits of the Kingdom, but few are willing to suffer to have them. This may be a hard pill to swallow, but Jesus suffered, and so will we.

Our optimism is not in the economy or our jobs and neither should it be in our own talents. Believers boast in the assured hope that Jesus promised to come back and get His church. In the meantime, we occupy until He comes. Areas of weakness in us individually or corporately are an invitation for deception and compromise, and it jeopardizes the whole.

With the decay in moral absolutes and gross darkness making its way upon the earth, Disciples must be able to wrestle with evil—and not be converted or consumed. We have to fight back without fear, endure and not faint, overcome and not be a victim, while maintaining spiritual integrity. Matthew 24 below outlines the future we will inevitably face, if we are not already:

- *For many will come in My name, saying, 'I am the Christ,' and will deceive many And you will hear of wars and rumors of wars. See that you are not troubled; for all these things must come to pass, but the end is not yet*
- *For nation will rise against nation, and kingdom against kingdom. And there will be famines, pestilences, and earthquakes in various places*
- *"Then they will deliver you up to tribulation and kill you, and you will be hated by all nations for My name's sake.*
- *And then many will be offended, will betray one another, and will hate one another. Then many false prophets will rise up and deceive many*
- *And because lawlessness will abound, the love of many will grow cold*

It goes on to say all these are the beginning of sorrows. This war is considered but a short affliction. A disciple's hope is not in things temporary, but toward what is eternal.

Lastly, becoming a disciple is not easy or for the faint of heart. We have to get the jelly out of our backbones. Do not think because we made a Romans 10:9 confession of faith and got baptized that we know how to pick up our cross and follow Him (Matthew 16:24). We have to be taught how to live as the Royal Priesthood and a peculiar people (1 Peter 2:9). It is a process that takes time, and it is the only way to get dislodged from the enemy's plot and cleave to God's plan.

No good thing will He withhold from those who walk uprightly (Psalm 84:11)

Section V

The Promise
Know Your Benefits Package

THE PROMISE

God Wants More for You

We are living in perilous times, and our ability to thrive in the inevitable chaos and uncertainty will be directly connected to our understanding and alignment with His promises. They are designed for us to experience Heaven on Earth. His benefits cover things we probably never thought about to help us avert spiritual demise.

It is important to understand the biblical constitution of His promises, and how His promises to Abraham affect us. His benefits package is strategic in aiding us against the deceptive campaign of the enemy. I will conclude with a pronouncement over you and a sampling of promises designed to keep you spiritually safe.

All born-again Christians—who are growing in grace—can indulge in over 3500 benefits. These incentives to righteousness are inherited once we get saved, and are now in our spiritual bank account. God wants us to have every spiritual blessing He has to offer. He is not slack concerning His promises (1 Peter 3:9). Every area of your life can be transformed by His goodness.

Oh, taste and see that the Lord is good; Blessed is the man who trusts in Him! Oh, fear the Lord, you His saints! There is no want to those who fear Him. The young lions lack and suffer hunger; But those who seek the Lord shall not lack any good thing (Psalm 34:8-10)

History Has Its Place

His promises are at our fingertips and Disciples can find great comfort in knowing them. Once we know what they are, the capacity to believe God for them may not be in our natural lineage, but it is certainly in our spiritual DNA. The purpose-driven lifestyle of Abraham will help us understand our inheritance; it sure did for me (Genesis 17:7).

God told the Patriarch, he and "all the families of the earth," which includes you, would be blessed (Genesis 12:2-3). It was through studying the ups and downs of Abraham's life, during a special season of being discipled, that I was able to grasp the importance of knowing His promises to me. God said, "I know what you need even before you ask." So, He sent me on a journey.

Many years ago, the Lord woke me up and impressed upon my heart to find *Rosh Hashanah* (The Jewish New Year) and *Yom Kippur* (The Day of Atonement and the holiest day of the year in Judaism) on the calendar.

In a nutshell, He wanted me to learn about the Jewish people so I could understand Him, as *The Promise*, better. There was no question I needed to be discipled on my spiritual lineage.

Since I am from the inner city, I could not imagine the journey I was about to take. My first thought was to befriend someone Jewish. Every time I met a Jewish person I shrilled with excitement trying to make a connection. You can probably imagine how well that went. Clearly, my vivacious demeanor was a bit much for the chosen crew.

One of His promises about direction is that He orders the steps of the righteous (Psalm 37:23). It was not long after He spoke to my heart that I found myself at a meeting of apostolic leaders. A friend insisted I meet one of the female apostles in San Diego. From the moment we met, I knew my life was about to change.

Although she is not Jewish, her character and conversation carried the familiar fragrance of His chosen people. She was as close to being Jewish as one could be who was not born and bred. God made promises to the Jews, but that Gentile Gal was going to get her inheritance and make sure I did too.

Apostle Billie, the *Shamar*, which means *Keeper of the Sabbath*, is the embodiment of the Old Testament's elegance and rituals, and the liberating grace of the New. She mastered taking religion out of the Feasts, First Fruits, and the celebration of the Sabbath.

She taught us how to grasp the revelation, not rituals, and bring it forward into our daily lives. It offered me an unimaginable season of healing, growth, and adoration for my Savior and King. Her devotion to Yeshua was an exquisite display of pageantry that made anyone want to lay at His feet.

Now, when I study the Scriptures, they are more alive. I recognize and comprehend things I never would have if I did not trust God and obey what He told me to do regarding learning about the High Holy days.

The season of being discipled by Apostle Billie was the precursor to me grasping the promise God made to Abraham and his seed—and in turn, the promise He made to me. As I learned more about my inheritance, through the Father of Faith, my confidence that His promises really were for me grew.

Because Abraham believed God, he was called righteous (Genesis 15:6). Because he trusted God, he was called the Father of Faith. But, these badges of distinction did not come without doubt, human reasoning, and failure. Just like I did, you too can learn from Abraham's life.

What he went through to see God's promises manifested through him was not easy, but every time he followed through, it was worth it. Here are some of the promises to Abraham and how they unfolded:

- He had to come from amongst the ungodly people and leave the comfort of his family (Genesis 12:1)—*Are you willing to do whatever it takes to receive your inheritance, even if that means you have to move?*
- God changed Abram's name to Abraham—*How would you handle a name change?*
- Abraham was promised an heir to inherit the land God gave him, but he and his wife Sarah were too old to conceive—*Do you believe God can do the impossible?*
  - It appeared, at least to Sarah, that God was taking too long so she solicited the help of Hagar, her slave girl, to have Abram's baby for her
  - Sometimes, we can be too smart for our own good—*the Father does not need our help to do what He tells us He is going to do. All He needs for us to do is believe*
  - Her gesture caused enough baby-mama drama to put the entire world at odds with Ishmael, Abraham's first-born son, who is not the son of the covenant
  - Now Ishmael and Isaac, who *is* the son of promise, give a new meaning to family feud and their descendants are still at odds today
- Abraham had to pass a great test of faith when in obedience to God; he was willing to sacrifice Isaac—*Do you love God enough to sacrifice what is important to you?*
  - God promised him a son, gave him one, and then he wanted him back
  - Actually, He really only wanted to see what Abraham would do—*at some point, God must know that our loyalty is to Him and not with what He can give us—every disciple will have a moment where our loyalty to God is established*

We are going to make mistakes, but know He is only disturbed by our rejection of His gifts. Even though God promised Abraham his dreams and unimaginable hopes, he wavered in his belief and in acting swiftly, but God still honored His Word to Abraham, and He wants to do the same with us. We only need to respond in faith to what He tells us, and allow Him to bless us.

A Little Goes A Long Way

The constitution of God's promises are preserved in the fact that He is not a man, and not only does He not lie, He cannot lie (Titus 1:2). He will always make good on His word (Numbers 23:19).

Twenty-some years ago, I did not know what I know today. The little that I did know may have saved my life. A verse kept coming back to me when the enemy, once again, was trying to steal my mind.

And we know that all things work together for good to those who love God, to those who are the called according to His purpose (Romans 8:28)

During the most difficult time of my life, I held on to His promise. I was drowning in devastation, grief, depression, and anxiety. The Planos spirits, or mind demons, were trying to take over. My mom's sudden death was so traumatizing, I eventually could not eat, walk, go to work, or think. Even crawling to the end of my bed was excruciating and exhausting.

Everything in me was shutting down. But, in the midst of the pain, His promise kept coming to my mind, and I would repeat it over and over again in my head. I told myself this was going to work out for my good. I could not see it then, but God said it would, and I believed it. I hummed that mantra until it became my reality.

Another thing I did during that time was whisper two words I used when talking to God, "You said." Now, no one can say, "You said," if we don't know what He said. Father loves it when His children remind Him of His word, because He delights in performing it (Jeremiah 1:12).

I suffered, cried a river of tears, took prescription pills, and wrestled with the loss to sheer exhaustion—but I never stopped believing. Eventually, the darkness receded, my health was restored, and I did not end up addicted to prescription drugs. God kept His promise.

Given to us exceedingly great and precious promises, that through these you
may be partakers of the divine nature, having escaped the corruption that is
in the world through lust (2 Peter 1:4)

When He makes a promise, He does not relent on them. His promises are not like ours. He is not prone to break His promises. Have you ever made a promise to someone that you did not keep? I have, and it is an awful feeling, especially when that promise is made to a child.

We have to raise the bar in keeping our word, because it is a sign of God's love perfected in us (1 John 2:5). His promises are His Word. They are not just letters written on a piece of paper. The ultimate promise God wants us to partake of is His promise of eternal life (1 John 2:25).

We do not have to worry about how the economy will affect God's ability to deliver on His Word. His promises are not connected to the corporate corruption on Wall Street, the unstable economy, or our unpredictable political system. Whether we can pay off the national debt or not does not matter. Neither are they connected to our righteousness or wickedness either.

Nothing that happens on the world scene can adversely affect what is betrothed to His beloved children. His promises cannot be stolen either. Finally, we should know His promises are not contingent upon us, but on the life of His son, Jesus Christ, in us.

Protection from the Enemy

The enemy has caused trouble since that day in the Garden, and He will continue to come after us, our families, resources, and anything else he can. There are promises that will help us be proactive, so we can dodge his attacks and defeat him.

One promise of protection is we can decree a thing and it shall be established (Job 22:28). Let's practice.

Father, thank you for your Word—powerful and mighty.
I speak promises of protection over your Beloved. Everything I decree, in
your name is established as your Word says it will be. Amen

Recite this aloud:

PROMISES OF PROTECTION DECREE

Today, I declare in the name of Jesus, that greater is He that is in you, than he that is in the world (1 John 4:4). God has not given you a Spirit of fear, but of power, and of love, and a sound mind (2 Timothy 1:7).

You have authority to trample on serpents and scorpions, and over all the power of the enemy, and nothing shall by any means hurt you (Luke 10:19). No weapon formed against you will prosper (Isaiah 54:17), and every tongue that rises up to attack you shall be silenced. God always gives you a way of escape (1 Corinthians 10:13).

Your enemies are defeated before your face, and they shall come out against you one way and flee before you seven (Deuteronomy 28:7). No one can snatch you out of His hand and you have the assurance the Lord watches over your coming and goings (Psalm 121:8). He is preparing a table for you in the presence of your enemies (Psalm 23:5).

I release the peace of God that surpasses all understanding, over you to know He will never leave you nor forsake you (Hebrews 13:5). He is your hedge of protection. Continue to resist the devil and he will flee, because greater is He that is in you than He that is in the world. We bind the strong man and cast down every stronghold.

In the name of Jesus, and by His blood, you will flourish in your walk with Him and fulfill your destiny. Receive it.

The promises of God make you a very wealthy person and they can keep you safe, but you have to claim them. Familiarize yourself with the ones you need, then go into your prayer closet and march boldly up to the throne where mercy is available in your time of need. In private, you can put a demand on your inheritance so you can be rewarded openly. God is waiting for your appearance. Do not let the promises He set aside for you go unclaimed.

So Jesus said to them again, "Peace to you! As the Father has sent Me, I also send you" (John 20:21)

Section VI

The Commissioning
Kingdom Activations

THE COMMISSIONING

Believers are called to live intentionally, not conveniently. Jesus lived the most extraordinary life any man could claim, and He expects you to live your best life too. There was nothing casual about His life, and the same can be true for us. Discipled Christians do not survive, they thrive. We should be getting brighter by the day. However, that will not happen if our only destination is the pew.

The pew is like the bleachers at a sporting event. They provide an awesome view of what is happening on the field. We feel part of every play, but we are not really in the game. Anybody can sit on the sideline and narrate the activities. God wants us off the pew and on the field where He can use us, and that is why we are being commissioned.

Being on the field is the real deal. It is exhilarating and exhausting, and nothing compares to it. Once we are in the game, we have conquered the biggest obstacle of all—the fear of failure. The only way to fail in the Kingdom is not to try.

The distance from where you are to where He wants you to be may appear too far to travel, especially if you feel unworthy. Seriously, are you kidding. Worthy? Who's worthy? None of us are worthy, so get over it.

A Man Given a Mission

No doubt, that had to be what Moses was thinking when God told Him He wanted him to lead His people: all 600,000 of them. Chances are, he panicked and had an anxiety attack. Maybe he wanted to do like Jonah and run to another city to hide.

Moses gave God every reason he could think of as to why He should pick someone else. He said he stuttered, he was a murderer, he had a quick temper and low self-esteem. As if God did not know these things before He knocked on his heart. If God were selecting people based on their abilities, none of us mere mortals would qualify.

Moses' commissioning was not about his abilities or lack of them. He was chosen, and so are you. What the Father wants to do—it will be Him doing it through you. God gave Moses whatever he needed to fulfill his assignment, and He has not changed.

Just like Moses, you might doubt, you will make mistakes, and you may even want to quit. I sure have. Then something awesome happens and you have to scream to Heaven that someone got saved, delivered, or healed. There will be moments when—if you are not leaping for joy, you will be tweeting how God allowed you to see miracles, signs, and wonders performed in your midst. Some of them you will even speak and call forth by faith yourself.

The Charge

The commissioning begins when we decide we want to grow. It is intended to release us into the spiritual activities we were saved to do. The only title we need to accomplish them is *servant.*

You will fulfill your commission if you are strategic and deliberate with your daily activities. It may take a little time to adjust to being evicted from your life, but you will get the hang of it with practice. You are about to embark upon an unnatural lifestyle saturated in obedience, grounded in giving, purposed in prayer, fueled by worship, seasoned in sacrifice, and sustained in love.

Nothing can be taken for granted, and all your encounters have to be vetted for relevance and direction. Recognize what commitments are casual, and which are covenant, and manage them accordingly. Each day is lived as if it is your last (Proverbs 27:1). Embrace these simple principals and your mouth should never taste of regret.

Now that you are no longer the owner, but a steward of your resources, they must be handled properly and placed purposely. It takes a Kingdom mentality to warden your life, your money, and your relationships according to Scripture.

Every good work is an opportunity to taste and see that the Lord is good. Your steps are ordered and they will take you where you need to go. Get over the need for a title, degree, ordination, or license. If you have one *great*, and if you want one, that is fine too. But, if you don't, *you are still an agent of the Kingdom.*

Special credentials are not necessary to do what Jesus told His disciples to do. Do not be stopped by commissioning killers like greed, slothfulness, doubt, pride, and unbelief.

What You Need for Your Commissioning

Another favorite verse of mine is *"For the kingdom of God is not in word but in power"* (1 Corinthians 4:20). Jesus shut down a lot of undermining agendas and ulterior motives when He demonstrated His power, and we must do the same. God's power is essential to doing His work.

You are perfect for this activation. It is the easiest way to get your feet wet. Take your rightful place in the Vineyard, and be who God created you to be. Do what He planned for you to do. Go where He intends on sending you. Say what He tells you to say. He wants nothing more than for you to flatter Him by following in His steps.

Once you renew your mind to the truth in His Word, and line up your thoughts with who He says you are, you are well on your way. Then you can build on that by learning your Kingdom responsibilities, choosing to mature in your character, and practice your gift(s).

Faith, combined with obedience, dissolves the deception that keeps us yoked to being perpetually inactive and spiritually unproductive. We really can break every chain. It is biblical to learn, grow, practice and then GO. It is not scriptural to get saved and sit still.

The yearning I felt while I sat consummated to that pew was so deep, it pierced the marrow in my bones. You are being tossed a spiritual lifejacket, which took years for me to get. There are enough activations on these pages alone to keep you occupied until Jesus parts the sky for His Second Coming.

Preparation for the Commissioning

There is no other body of people who has the power we do to make the world a better place. We are instruments of transformation, elevation, and activation. Your birth was purposed. You might have been an accident for your mama or your daddy, but God does not make mistakes.

This is your OJT (on the job training). You are about to do exactly what Jesus did with the disciples. He put them to work, and they grew into maturity in the process, which was considered normal.

Now, before you make a mad dash out of the pew, keep in mind that God has no interest in you doing His bidding at the expense of your family's well being. To honor your family is your first commission. He frowns when you neglect your home, your spouse, your children, or your worldly responsibilities. When you dishonor them, you dishonor Him. He has made a way for us to do both, and that is decent and in order.

If you are concerned about growing in your faith through this commissioning, talk to God. Also ask Him to reveal anything hidden that would hold you back. His specialty is to give us strategy to overcome every obstacle to taking action. He will also go before you and make the crooked places straight (Isaiah 45:2). It is His good pleasure to honor His Word—and our responsibility is to trust Him.

In the Kingdom of God, one day is as a thousand years, but here time is short, so use it wisely. We cannot make up for time squandered, but God's promise is to redeem what was stolen. Do not tarry, the harvest is plentiful and the laborers are few and we have a lot of work to do.

ACTIVATIONS *(Check all that apply.)*

MANDATORY PRE-REQUISITE TO ALL ACTIVATIONS
The New Covenant Commandments (Matthew 22:37)
❑#1 - LOVE GOD with all your heart, soul, mind, and all your strength
❑#2 - LOVE YOUR NEIGHBOR as you want to be loved

FOUNDATIONAL COMMISSIONING:
❑ **BECOME A DISCIPLE** and compare yourself to no one, but Christ; you will go through a process of realignment in every area of your life; your priorities will be re-arranged and so will your money; He will begin to shift every part of you to His Word

Activations for All Believers

❑ **CORRECT ALL DISOBEDIENCE**—If there is anything you know God told you to do, do it. This is your first order of business. Nothing else can be accomplished until this is handled. Disobedience is rebellion and rebellion is as witchcraft (1 Samuel 15:23). This activation alone will shift the entire family of God to another level
❑ **ACCEPT YOUR CALL TO THE MINISTRY** If God has called you into the ministry say yes today and then tell someone what you did

❑ **GRADUATE FROM THE PEW** by making a conscious effort to do more than just go to church, and then encourage someone else to do it too

❑ **FIND YOUR PLACE IN THE KINGDOM** and step into it

❑ **GET ACTIVE IN YOUR LOCAL CHURCH** and if you don't have one find one

❑ **BE THE CHURCH** everywhere you go, not only on Sundays

❑ **GET SPIRIT-FILLED** because without Him, you are fighting a losing battle; read your Bible and learn about this requirement for yourself (Acts 1:5, Acts 2:38, Matthew 3:11, John 3:5, Acts 2:4)

❑ **BUILD YOUR SKILL** in evangelism

❑ **TELL PEOPLE ABOUT JESUS** and give them the Good News, not a conditional gospel

❑ **RETURN TO THE CHURCH** if you severed your relationship with the family of God

❑ **STEP OUT IN FAITH** and pray for someone who is sick

❑ **LEARN HOW TO CAST OUT DEMONS** and practice self-deliverance visit www.hardcorechristianity.com and click on the deliverance button

❑ **STOP MAKING EXCUSES** for living a righteous and holy life

❑ **HONOR YOUR MOTHER AND FATHER** and break the curse that comes from dishonoring your parents

❑ **HUSBANDS LOVE YOUR WIVES** so your prayers can be heard

❑ **WIVES RESPECT YOUR HUSBANDS,** no excuses

❑ **FORGIVE** everyone, for anything, no matter what they did or said, so you can be forgiven (Matthew 6:14-15)

❑ **READ AND STUDY YOUR BIBLE** daily

❑ **INVITE SOMEONE TO CHURCH** no matter how long it takes, and then do it again

❑ **DISCIPLE ANOTHER PERSON** intentionally to grow the Kingdom exponentially

❑ **LEARN** the basics about being a Believer (i.e. spirit-and-water baptism, giving, communion, healing, gifts, forgiveness, etc.)

❑ **PRACTICE** worship at home

❑ **FIND A SPIRITUAL ENTREPRENUER** and partner with them in prayer, contributions, human capital and/or referrals

❑ **SCHEDULE A MISSIONS TRIP** locally or abroad, or support someone who does mission's and do it with your family, friends or colleagues

❑ **PRAY** FOR OUR RELIGIOUS AND WORLD LEADERS
❑ **HELP A CHILD** Activations (Let God lead you)

___SHARE the Good News of Jesus Christ with a child

___READ the Bible to a child

___DISCIPLE a child

___RAISE a child with reverence for God

___RESTORE your relationship with a child, even if that child has become an adult

___ENCOURAGE a child every chance you get

___BECOME a foster parent and share God's love with a displaced child in need

___ADOPT a child and give them a Christian home because thousands of children are waiting

___TAKE a child in your family or neighborhood to church

___DO a bible study in your home for children

___DONATE to anything that helps a child

___BUILD a business with a child

___TEACH Sunday School at your church

___RECOGNIZE or help develop a child's spiritual gift(s) and/or natural talents

___MENTOR a child

___VOLUNTEER for an organization that helps foster children and/or orphans locally, nationally or internationally

___REPORT child abuse or neglect immediately

___FRIEND a family with children and bring the Kingdom of Heaven to earth for them

___SUPPORT children in any way you can

___PRAY for our children, all 1.9 billion of them

Finally, these are activations that will eject you from the pew, destroy the works of the enemy, and bring the Kingdom of Heaven to Earth (Luke 10:9). Of course, this is not possible in your own strength, but by His Spirit. What are you waiting for?

Log on to www.disciplemenow.com for more activations and to share your activation success stories.

Therefore, if anyone is in Christ, he is a new creation; old things have passed away; behold, all things have become new (2 Corinthians 5:17)

Section VII

THE CONCLUSION
New Beginnings

THE CONCLUSION

Congratulations. You did it. You finished the book. No doubt your spiritual real estate in the Kingdom has gone up, and you now have the tools to be a lethal threat to the enemy. Will you use them?

It is exciting to know that all of heaven rejoiced when you made your confession of faith. Now, Jesus—who is your advocate—is sitting at the right hand of the Father discussing your next move to become a mature disciple. Make a conscious choice to come off the pew, and boldly step into an unapologetic life as a true servant of the King. It is the single most amazing thing you will ever do.

We are His people and the sheep of His pasture. There is nothing He won't do for us, especially when we are on one accord. When Christians are lined up biblically, connected properly, and acting righteously, we are the most powerful people on the planet. The truth is, nothing can stop us from becoming who He died for us to be, unless we let it.

He will not disappoint you, like so many others have. Your name is in the registry of the redeemed called the Book of Life, and that means something. Not to mention there is a crown with your name on it.

We were saved to be a conduit for the Kingdom of God, to come to earth as it is in Heaven. This path provides a river of living water that quenches your thirst to be fulfilled, and it fans the flames of fire that cause revival to spring forth out of your belly. Living the life you were destined for is truly unimaginable and I am speaking from experience. Unfruitful tradition, complacency, and mediocrity can end instantly if you humbly come into alignment with God's wisdom.

- **The problem** is only an opportunity
- **The plot** can be overcome
- **The plan** is simple: become a disciple
- **The players** are necessary
- **The promise** is waiting
- **The commissioning** is the activation you longed for

Although turbulent times are coming, **Revival in the Pews** reveals what it takes to endure, overcome, and be victorious as biblical prophecies unfold. We are not victims, we are victorious. One by one, we can transform our own lives with the truth, and then we can multiply. Take what you have been gifted within these pages, make the appropriate corrections, and then pass it along. You can walk in unprecedented victory.

We serve a patient God who is merciful in His waiting for us to turn toward Him (2 Peter 3:9). He never intended for your salvation experience to be uneventful, un-impactful, or unrewarding. Your life as a Christian does not have to be substandard because of your past, the condition of the church, or the complacency of anyone around you. Jesus set the example for you to follow. If He could do what He was commissioned to do, and fulfilled His destiny, you can too.

Now, run to the altar of your heart and disclose your disappointments, admit your transgressions, lay down your cross, and pick up His. Let God ignite a fire inside of you that can never be quenched. He will meet you at the door of your confession, the place where love conquers all. Mercy will consume your failures, grace will fuel your future, and His unconditional love will change and guide you to places you never dreamed. He anxiously waits, like a chivalrous gentleman holding open the door for His Beloved.

Additional Resources

ARIZONA DELIVERANCE CENTER (ADC) aka Hardcore Christianity and House of Healing
Founder, Michael W. Smith—certified professional counselor with thirty-five plus years of experience.

ADC is a non-denominational, non-profit 501(c)(3) Christian discipleship training center for healing, inner healing, evangelism, and deliverance. HCC is dedicated to providing free counseling services to the poor and helping individuals who are afflicted by mental illness, physical illness, emotional illness, and spiritual oppression.

Website: www.hardcorechristianity.com

Free deliverance services every Tuesday – Friday night at seven.

Watch all services via Livestream: http://original.livestream.com/hohaz

13342 N. 15th Avenue – Phoenix, Arizona 85015

Mailing Address: P.O. Box 1116 - Sun City, Arizona 85372

Ministry Line 602-636-5800

Self-deliverance Instructions: http://www.hardcorechristianity.com/index.php?page=14

24/7 Free Online Teachings:
- YouTube: Houseofhealingaz
- YouTube: Hardcore Christianity Deliverance Training Channel
- YouTube: Hardcore Christianity Video Training Channel
- Radio Program 24/7: soundcloud.com/hardcore-Christianity

KXXT/1010AM, M-F @ 7:30 AM, KXEG/1280AM, M-F at 7:00 AM, Arizona time

Facebook: Hardcorechristianity.com

Submit online deliverance prayer requests: http://www.hardcorechristianity.com/index.php?page=7

Make a tax-deductible donation to help build the Arizona Deliverance Center: http://www.hardcorechristianity.com/index.php?page=22

JUDY BAUER MINISTRIES

Website: www.jbmnow.org

The Father's Family Business: http://www.kamtraining4u.com/

Spiritual Life Strategies - http://www.judybauer.org/

Spiritual Entrepreneurs - http://www.kamnationhub.org/

Free Weekly Devotional: https://jbmkam.leadpages.co/tues-devo/

Email: judy@jbmnow.org

Appendix

(Endnotes)

1   "What is Christian revival?," *Got Questions Ministries*, http://www.gotquestions.org/Christian-revival.html

2   Dr. Richard J. Krejcir, "Statistics and Reasons for Church Decline," *ChurchLeadership.org*, 2007, http://www.churchleadership.org/apps/articles/default.asp?articleid=42346&columnid=4545

3   "Missions Education," *One World Missions*, http://oneworldmissions.com/site.cfm?PageID=5521

4   http://www.answers.com/Q/How_many_Christians_are_there_worldwide

5   Lyn Mize, "Soul vs Spirit Salvation," *First Fruits Ministry*, www.ffruits.org/v03/soulvsspiritsalvation.html

6   Gaines R. Johnson, "Understanding the Biblical Difference Between the Words *World* and Earth," *The Bible Genesis & Geology*, www.kjvbible.org/theworlds.html

7   http://av1611.com/kjbp/kjv-dictionary/pride.html

8   The Barna Group, "Most American Christians Do Not Believe that Satan or the Holy Spirit Exist," *Barna.com*, April 13, 2009, https://www.barna.com/research/most-american-christians-do-not-believe-that-satan-or-the-holy-spirit-exist/

9   Graeme Goldsworthy *"Gospel and Kingdom: A Christian Interpretation of the Old Testament,"* Theopedia, p. 53, http://www.theopedia.com/graeme-goldsworthy

10   https://www.justice.gov/sites/default/files/eoir/legacy/2013/06/11/economic%20conditions.pdf

11   *Maldonado, Guillermo, The Kingdom of Power: How to Demonstrate It Here & Now, Whitaker House, 2013*

12   What is the kingdom of God?, "Gotquestions.org," *God Questions Ministries*, http://www.gotquestions.org/kingdom-of-God.html

13 Charles E. Hackett, "Alarming Statistics," *Crosswalk.com*, April 7, 4002, http://www.crosswalk.com/church/pastors-or-leadership/alarming-statistics-1256307.html

14 Allen Ross, "The Religious World of Jesus," *Bible.org*, April 12, 2006, https://bible.org/seriespage/7-scribes

15 J. Julius Scott, Jr., "Baker's Evangelical Dictionary of Biblical Theology," *Bible-studytools.com*, http://www.biblestudytools.com/dictionary/pharisees/

16 Caleb K. Bell, "Poll: Americans love the Bible but don't read it much," *Religion News Service,* April 4, 2013, http://religionnews.com/2013/04/04/poll-americans-love-the-bible-but-dont-read-it-much/

17 Dr. Richard J. Krejcir, "Statistics and Reasons for Church Decline," *Churchleadership.org*, 2007, http://www.churchleadership.org/apps/articles/default.asp?articleid=42346&columnid=4545

18 Dr. Richard J. Krejcir, "Statistics and Reasons for Church Decline," *Churchleadership.org*, 2007, http://www.churchleadership.org/apps/articles/default.asp?articleid=42346&columnid=4545

19 Wikipedia contributors, "Kundalini," *Wikipedia*, The Free Encyclopedia, https://en.wikipedia.org/w/index.php?title=Kundalini&oldid=757055880 (accessed December 28, 2016)

20 Wikipedia contributors, "Kundalini," *Wikipedia*, The Free Encyclopedia, https://en.wikipedia.org/w/index.php?title=Kundalini&oldid=743749954 (accessed October 11, 2016).

21 Barna Group, "New Research on the State of Discipleship," *Barna.com*, December 1, 2015, https://www.barna.com/research/new-research-on-the-state-of-discipleship/

22 Barna Group, "New Research on the State of Discipleship," *Barna.com*, December 1, 2015, https://www.barna.com/research/new-research-on-the-state-of-discipleship/

23 Dr. Richard J. Krejcir, "Statistics and Reasons for Church Decline," *Churchleadership.org*, 2007, http://www.churchleadership.org/apps/articles/default.asp?articleid=42346&columnid=4545

24 Dr. Richard J. Krejcir, "Statistics and Reasons for Church Decline," *Churchleadership.org*, 2007, http://www.churchleadership.org/apps/articles/default.asp?articleid=42346&columnid=4545

Made in the USA
San Bernardino, CA
05 March 2018